# A Century of Free Speech at the City Club of Cleveland

# The Creed of the City Club

I HAIL and harbor and hear
men of every belief and party; for within my portals prejudice grows
less and bias dwindles.

I have a forum—as wholly uncensored as it is rigidly impartial.
'Freedom of Speech' is graven above my rostrum; and beside
it 'Fairness of Speech.'

I am the product of the people, a cross section of their community—
weak as they are weak, and strong in their strength;
believing that knowledge of our failings and our powers begets
a greater strength. I have a house of fellowship; under my
roof informality reigns and strangers need no introduction.

I welcome to my platform the discussion of any theory or
dogma of reform; but I bind my household to the espousal of
none of them, for I cherish the freedom of every man's conviction and
each of my kin retains his own responsibility.

I have no axe to grind, no logs to roll. My abode shall be the
rendezvous of strong but open-minded men and my watchword
shall be 'information,' not 'reformation.'

I am accessible to men of all sides—literally and figuratively—
for I am located in the heart of a city—spiritually and geographically.

I am the city's club—The City Club.


—Ralph A. Hayes (1916)

The writing and publication of this book
have been generously underwritten by a grant
from the Abington Foundation.


The printing of this book was contributed by
Consolidated Solutions of Cleveland.

Carol Poh

# A Century of Free Speech at the City Club of Cleveland

 THE CITY CLUB OF CLEVELAND

© 2014 The City Club of Cleveland

All rights reserved. Published 2014
Printed in the United States of America

Unless otherwise noted, all photographs in
Part Two: The Forum are by Sam Adamo.

Designed by Thomas Barnard

Printed by Consolidated Graphics Group, Inc. of Cleveland

ISBN: 978-0-615-99349-2

The City Club of Cleveland
850 Euclid Avenue
Cleveland, Ohio 44114

www.cityclub.org
216-621-0082

Library of Congress Control Number: 2014936281

Free speech is the whole thing, the whole ball game. Free speech is life itself.

—Salman Rushdie

## Contents

xi    Foreword by John Glenn

xiii    Preface and Acknowledgements

**1**    **Part One: THE CLUB**

The City Club of Cleveland Turns One Hundred

**54**    **Part Two: THE FORUM**

Memorable Speeches, 1987–2012

58    Justice Sandra Day O'Connor *February 10, 1987*

62    President Ronald Reagan *January 11, 1988*

66    Pei Min Xin *June 9, 1989*

71    William Sloane Coffin *May 4, 1990*

74    Lester Thurow *November 1, 1991*

78    Russell Means *December 11, 1992*

82    Debate: Lieutenant Tracy Thorne vs. Major General James Milnor Roberts *February 26, 1993*

86    President Bill Clinton *October 24, 1994*

90    House Speaker Newt Gingrich *July 31, 1995*

94    Gerda Weissmann Klein and Kurt Klein *November 15, 1996*

98    Rita Dove and Henry Louis Gates Jr. *May 9, 1997*

102    Marian Wright Edelman *October 3, 1998*

106    Louis Stokes *June 30, 1999*

110    David S. Broder *May 12, 2000*

114    William A. McDonough *April 20, 2001*

118    Hassan Abdel Rahman *May 10, 2002*

122    John Glenn *August 29, 2003*

126    Condoleezza Rice *October 15, 2004*

130    Anne Mulcahy *March 11, 2005*

134    President George W. Bush *March 20, 2006*

138    Geoffrey Canada *December 3, 2007*

142    Jim Rokakis *May 28, 2008*

146    Sister Helen Prejean *September 18, 2009*

150    Representative John A. Boehner *August 24, 2010*

154    Alan K. Simpson *November 18, 2011*

158    Ted Turner *May 18, 2012*

163    Appendix I: Historical Timeline of the City Club of Cleveland

166    Appendix II: Presidents of the City Club of Cleveland

167    Appendix III: Chief Executives of the City Club of Cleveland

169    A Note on Sources

171    Index of Names

**Foreword**

People have wondered about freedom all through the ages, but it was left for the Fathers of the American Constitution to draft a working document to make it all happen. It was not an easy concept to execute. In fact, it turned out to outline one of the most complex forms of government ever conceived, but also the best.

Its rock-bottom foundation, however, rests on the participation of all our citizens to make the decisions of leadership and major issues, with every person's vote being equal in determining the future of this continuing experiment in democracy, without regard to economic or social status.

The City Club throughout its 100-year history has provided a way of keeping people informed so those decisions will be made with the best information possible. That is crucial in our democracy, for success depends on participation by all.

Congratulations to the City Club and best wishes in keeping us all better informed!

Senator John Glenn (Ret.)

## Preface and Acknowledgements

This project offered an extraordinary opportunity for a writer who has devoted nearly four decades to mining and writing about the history of my adopted hometown of Cleveland. In November 2011, as the 100th anniversary of the City Club of Cleveland approached, a committee charged with producing a book to mark the occasion invited me to discuss the project and propose a concept. Although I am not a member of the City Club, over the years I have listened to innumerable broadcasts of the City Club Forum and was well aware of its fine reputation and the high caliber of its speakers.

The present effort springs from and complements two earlier volumes: *Freedom's Forum: The City Club 1912–1962*, by Thomas F. Campbell, and *America's Soapbox: Seventy-five Years of Free Speaking at Cleveland's City Club Forum*, by Mark Gottlieb and Diana Tittle. Part One tells the story of a "social club with a civic purpose" founded in 1912 by young progressives when Cleveland, the nation's "Sixth City," was a formidable industrial and economic power. It describes how that club matured to reflect a changing city and nation. It is decidedly an essay, *not* a history, and contains few footnotes, although a note at the back of the book identifies the principal sources of the information presented. Part Two offers up-close encounters with the renowned City Club Forum in the years since the club marked its seventy-fifth anniversary. As a whole, the book attempts to fulfill the objective articulated by one member of the book committee—"It should say, 'Look what we've become'"—and demonstrates that, in the words of another member, "the City Club of Cleveland has evolved to meet the modern world."

I would like to thank the members of the centennial book committee for the time and attention they devoted to this project: Chairman Rick Taft, Len Calabrese, Dennis Dooley, Jim Foster, and Bob Lustig. It was they who sifted through a quarter-century of forum speeches to select those speakers to be profiled and the many others deserving of mention. For two decades of that quarter-century, Jim Foster served as executive director of the City Club. Each of the other gentlemen is a longtime City Club member and former president. Together, committee members brought a deep institutional knowledge to the project. Each reviewed and commented on the manuscript as it evolved. Dennis Dooley, a veteran writer and editor, went a step further, putting his red pen to the text, tightening and brightening my prose. Rick Taft, who in thirty-six years of club membership has rarely missed a Friday forum, collaborated closely on the speaker profiles, offering astute comments for my consideration before we shared drafts with the rest of the committee. With significant help from Jim Foster and City Club staff member Gary Musselman, he also took upon himself the daunting task of scouring the club's photographic records to assemble the many speaker images in Part Two.

I would also like to thank the many members of the City Club who participated in personal interviews. They are: Stanley Adelstein (who also read and commented on an early draft of the essay), Bruce Akers, Rena Blumberg Olshansky, Len Calabrese, Robert Conrad, Nancy Cronin, Dennis Dooley, Bob Lustig, Richard Pogue, Roberta Steinbacher, Louis Stokes, and Rick Taft. Lillian Anderson, who worked closely with Alan Davis during his tenure as executive director, also sat down for a personal interview, as did Jim Foster and Dan Moulthrop, who was named CEO of the club in 2013. Fred Vierow, a former club secretary, kindly shared his recollections by telephone, as did longtime member Art Brooks.

I am in debt as well to several staff members of the City Club. Elizabeth Horrigan, director of the club's 100th anniversary celebration, expertly coordinated the book project in its early months. Gary Musselman provided guidance to the club's files, delivered impossibly heavy cartons of old scrapbooks and documents retrieved from offsite storage, and diligently searched for pertinent photographs. Michael Crimaldi supplied DVDs of the forum speeches profiled here and responded to myriad requests, while Sam Adamo's engaging portraits of forum speakers, made during his thirty-three-year association with the club, considerably enhance Part Two.

I am grateful to David Goldberg, a professor of history at Cleveland State University, for reading a draft of Part One through the lens of his expertise and offering helpful comments. Marguerite Campbell shared her husband Tom Campbell's 1972 speech (extensively quoted in the essay) advocating the admission of women to membership in the City Club. Jewel Moulthrop copyedited the manuscript. Lastly, I appreciate the kind assistance of those who conserve and made available the many historic photographs that grace Part One: Margaret Baughman at the Cleveland Public Library, Lynn Duchez Bycko at the Michael Schwartz Library of Cleveland State University, and Ann K. Sindelar and Vicki Catozza at the Western Reserve Historical Society Library.

Carol Poh
Cleveland, Ohio
June 2014

# Part One
## The Club

1. Cleveland, the "Sixth City," about 1910. From 1912 until 1916, the City Club occupied the second and third floors of Weber's restaurant on Superior Avenue, just off Public Square. The building, with its distinctive stepped gables, can be seen here in the row of low-rise buildings to the right of the United States Courthouse. LIBRARY OF CONGRESS

Weber's restaurant, the first home of the City Club

1

# "Mr. President"

# The City Club of Cleveland Turns One Hundred

On Monday, March 20, 2006, President George W. Bush appeared before the City Club of Cleveland, where he made a speech designed to shore up flagging public support for the war in Iraq. Addressing a large audience at the Renaissance Cleveland Hotel on Public Square, he described the coalition's recent success in the northern Iraqi city of Tal Afar, once a key base for Al Qaeda, where a new strategy of "clear, hold, and build" had re-established order. The example of Tal Afar, the president said, "gives reason for hope of a free Iraq."

In the question-and-answer period that followed, Stanley Adelstein, a longtime City Club member, raised his hand and was recognized. "Mr. President," he began, "at the beginning of your talk today you mentioned that you understand why Americans have had their confidence shaken by the events in Iraq." He continued:

> Before we went to war in Iraq, you said that there were three main reasons for going to war: weapons of mass destruction, the claim that Iraq was sponsoring the terrorists who had attacked us on 9/11, and that Iraq had purchased nuclear materials from Niger. All three of those turned out to be false. My question is: How do we restore confidence in our leaders, so that Americans can be sure that the information they're getting now is correct?

Momentarily nonplussed, President Bush denied that he had ever said there was a connection between Saddam Hussein and 9/11, calling it a "misperception," but admitted "we were wrong on the intelligence."

Such unscripted discourse is de rigueur at the City Club of Cleveland, where speakers are expected to articulate— and defend—their ideas. No moderator intervenes; questions are unscreened and authentic. Club members and guests simply raise their hands to be heard. Thus does the City Club of Cleveland foster and defend free speech not only from the podium, but also from the floor. As one City Club member has observed, "Speech and questions form the call and response of democracy, the process of kaleidoscopic inquiry which helps decide to what ideas, and to what people, the governed will give their consent."[1]

President George W. Bush

## A "social club with a civic purpose"

The City Club of Cleveland was conceived amid the intellectual ferment of the Progressive Era, a period of social and political reform that, in Cleveland, reached its apogee during Tom L. Johnson's four terms as mayor (1901–09). Johnson attracted the best and the brightest to his administration, spoke directly to immigrants and the unlettered in his

1. "What Is a Great Question?" Remarks of Rick Taft on the occasion of his induction, with his father, Seth Taft, into the City Club of Cleveland Hall of Fame, April 19, 2004.

Mayo Fesler, 1911. Fesler conceived the idea of a "city club" for Cleveland, modeling it on one in St. Louis, and served as its first (unpaid) secretary. THE CLEVELAND PRESS COLLECTION, MICHAEL SCHWARTZ LIBRARY, CLEVELAND STATE UNIVERSITY

famous "tent" meetings, and initiated an array of public-welfare improvements that led the journalist Lincoln Steffens, in 1905, to hail him as "the best mayor of the best governed city in America." Some of those who served this progressive mayor—including Newton D. Baker, who himself would be elected mayor of Cleveland in 1912 and later go on to serve as President Woodrow Wilson's secretary of war—helped organize the City Club and sustained it in its early years.

The seed for the City Club was planted by an idealistic young reformer named Mayo Fesler, who was working as the secretary of the Municipal Association. Before coming to Cleveland, Fesler had been a member of a club in St. Louis that he viewed as a model for a comparable enterprise in Cleveland. On June 14, 1912, together with Augustus R. Hatton, a professor of political science at Western Reserve University, Fesler invited a group of civic-minded young men to meet over lunch at the Chamber of Commerce. Fesler arranged for several visitors in town from Boston, Chicago, and St. Louis to join them to share their experiences with city clubs in those cities. Six weeks later, a committee formed to study the matter reported affirmatively. "A city club will furnish a meeting place for men of all shades of opinions, political beliefs and social relations," it wrote, adding that "accurate information on public questions is a fundamental need in all our cities, and . . . a free, open discussion of these problems is the most effective way of securing and disseminating such information."

The City Club of Cleveland Company was incorporated under the laws of Ohio on October 27, 1912. Five men signed the articles of incorporation: H. Melvin Roberts, Walter L. Flory, Edward M. Baker, John A. Alburn, and Mayo Fesler. Article three declared the club's purpose:

> Said corporation is formed for the purpose of investigation, discussion and improvement of civic conditions and affairs in Cleveland; the maintenance of club rooms, library and other facilities of a social club for the use of men desiring to co-operate in the furtherance of these objects; the arrangement of frequent meetings, at which speakers may be heard and questions of civic interest may be discussed.

Daniel E. Morgan, a prominent attorney, was a founder and the first president of the City Club. He later served as a state senator, Cleveland city manager, and a judge on the Court of Appeals. This depiction of him appeared in the book *Cleveland Club Men in Caricature* (1910).

2. In 1925, the Internal Revenue Service granted the City Club of Cleveland 501(c)(4) status as a civic league pursuing social welfare rather than financial gain. This meant it would owe no taxes on income related to its civic work. In 1977, the club modified its Ohio articles of incorporation to shift from for-profit to not-for-profit status. In 1996, the IRS determined that the club qualified as a 501(c)(3) charitable/educational organization to which donors could make tax-deductible contributions.

The City Club was chartered as a for-profit corporation; its capital stock was set at $10,000, divided into one thousand shares valued at $10 each. One hundred and sixty-five men were invited to attend the organizational meeting of a "social club with a civic purpose." The meeting was held at the Chamber of Commerce building on Public Square on October 30. With Daniel E. Morgan presiding, Mayor Newton D. Baker, Judge Frederick A. Henry, and Professor Hatton each elaborated on the need for such a club, following which the subscription books were opened and seventy-eight subscribers purchased one share each.[2]

The roster of the City Club's founding members and first directors included many of those active in the city's social and political reform movements. In addition to Mayor Baker, Daniel Morgan, Judge Henry, and Professor Hatton, they included Arthur Baldwin, an attorney and founder of the Legal Aid Society of Cleveland; Rabbi Moses J. Gries, a proponent of Reform Judaism and spiritual leader of Temple Tifereth Israel (The Temple); broker and philanthropist

Toledo Mayor Brand Whitlock, here flanked by Mayors Henry Thomas Hunt of Cincinnati (at left) and Newton D. Baker of Cleveland, addressed the first City Club Forum, on December 21, 1912. Although the photograph is undated, all three men attended a conference sponsored by the Municipal Association of Cleveland held in Columbus, Ohio, in January 1912. Baker, a founder of the City Club of Cleveland, served two terms as mayor of Cleveland, following which he was tapped by President Woodrow Wilson to serve as secretary of war. LIBRARY OF CONGRESS

Edward M. Baker; attorney Alfred A. Benesch, who was elected to the city council in 1912 and two years later was tapped by Mayor Baker to serve as city safety director; federal bankruptcy referee Carl D. Friebolin; social worker Starr Cadwallader, and *Cleveland Plain Dealer* editor Erie C. Hopwood. Daniel Morgan (who would later serve as city manager during Cleveland's brief experiment with the city manager form of government) was elected to a one-year term as the club's first president, and Mayo Fesler agreed to continue as the club's interim, unpaid secretary.

The principal activity of the City Club was to be luncheon forums featuring distinguished guest speakers, followed by a question-and-answer period. The general format for these programs has never changed. Until the 1960s, the club followed a seasonal schedule, holding forums each Saturday at one o'clock from September or October through May. It was not yet the era of the five-day work week; most business and professional men worked downtown and put in time at their offices on Saturdays.

Club members' keen interest in municipal affairs was evident from the beginning. The first forum, held on December 21, 1912, in the assembly room of the Hollenden Hotel, featured a talk by Brand Whitlock, the reform mayor of Toledo. Other programs in the club's short inaugural season (held in various venues while the club searched for a permanent home) included a debate on street transportation between Street Railroad Commissioner Peter Witt and subway proponent William R. Hopkins; a panel discussion on the question "Shall Cleveland Have a New Charter?"; a presentation on "The Child Labor Problem" featuring the secretary of the National Child Labor Committee; and a talk by Werner Hegemann, a city planner and architecture critic visiting from Berlin (who pronounced Cleveland too small to support a subway). It is interesting to note that women, although excluded from membership, occasionally appeared as forum speakers, and whenever a particular program was deemed to be of interest to women—such as the one on child labor and another, in November 1913, on social-center and playground development—club members were permitted to bring women as guests.

In May 1913, the City Club established its first home above Weber's restaurant, just off Public Square on the south side of Superior Avenue and kitty-corner from City Hall. The club dining room was on the second floor. Clubrooms—where members might play a game of pool or read one of the many newspapers and magazines scattered on the library table—were on the third. "The atmosphere," Thomas F. Campbell wrote in *Freedom's Forum*, a history of the City Club published in 1963, "was one of warm fellowship cemented by a common interest in civic affairs and a hypnotic fascination with politics."

With a new home and an array of interesting programs, the City Club's public profile grew quickly. The Saturday forums comprised a mixture of local speakers addressing contemporary civic issues and visitors of national and even international stature. The Cuyahoga County engineer described plans for the Detroit-Superior High-Level Bridge, the president of the Cleveland Electric Illuminating Company argued against the municipal ownership of utilities (even as the city moved forward with plans for a municipal electric plant), and the mayors of six cities and villages adjoining Cleveland, together with Cleveland Mayor Harry L. Davis, presented their views on annexation. Lucy Price of the National Association Opposed to Woman Suffrage and Florence E. Allen, representing the Ohio Woman Suffrage Association, debated the Nineteenth Amendment.[3]

The City Club opened its third forum season on Monday, September 28, 1914, having scored a major coup: it was to host former President Theodore Roosevelt. In anticipation of a large audience, the club arranged for Mr. Roosevelt to speak in the auditorium of the Chamber of Commerce on Public Square. Secretary Fesler allocated two tickets for each City Club member—one for his use, the other for a guest. Arriving in Cleveland after spending two days at the Mentor, Ohio, home of James R. Garfield,[4] Roosevelt addressed an audience of 1,500. He flayed "wet" politicians, speaking against a proposal to amend the state constitution to establish home rule in the regulation of liquor traffic, and advocated giving women the right to vote. Page one of

> **The City Club opened its third forum season on Monday, September 28, 1914, having scored a major coup: it was to host former President Theodore Roosevelt.**

the next day's *Cleveland Plain Dealer* featured an extended account of Roosevelt's visit accompanied by a half-dozen caricatures, including one depicting City Club President John H. Clarke introducing the former president. The young club could not have received better publicity: T.R.'s appearance not only boosted the City Club's profile locally, but also carried its name far beyond Cleveland.

As membership grew, the City Club became a much sought-after platform for a wide variety of speakers. The club hosted George Lansbury, a British social reformer who would later lead the Labour Party, and Count Mihály Károlyi, who came to build support for Hungary's independence. In February 1915, in the first of three appearances he would make at the City Club, W. E. B. Du Bois spoke on the subject of "War and Race Prejudice." The foremost black intellectual of his time, Du Bois contended that the war in Europe would lessen racial prejudice and broaden democracy, "which has heretofore existed only for the white races."

Membership stood at 925 when, at the end of March 1916, club President Augustus Hatton boasted to the *Plain Dealer* that "the new members come from every conceivable walk of life. The club is realizing its ambition of becoming a cross-section of the community." This was hardly true, of course. The City Club, in fact, comprised largely white middle-class business and professional men who made their living in or near downtown Cleveland, then the nation's sixth-largest city. The club was top-heavy with lawyers (235), followed by sizeable numbers of salesmen (68), instructors (56), manufacturers (45), bankers and brokers (42), physicians (40), real estate men (40), professors (17), judges (14), company presidents (10), and architects (10). They came to lunch with friends as they engaged in debate or stimulating conversation. During the forum season, they came on Saturdays to hear an interesting and sometimes provocative speaker, and then ply him (occasionally her) with questions.

3. In 1922, Allen would return to speak to the City Club as the first woman to serve on the Ohio Supreme Court.

4. Garfield, a member of the City Club who had served as Roosevelt's secretary of the interior, was then running for Governor of Ohio on the Progressive Party ticket.

Ralph A. Hayes (1894–1977) was the first paid secretary of the City Club and the author of its creed. A native of Crestline, Ohio, Hayes left Cleveland in 1916 to become personal secretary to Newton D. Baker, U.S. secretary of war. An effective administrator with a talent for connecting affluent people with charitable causes, he later became the first director of the New York Community Trust and remained on its board for more than forty years. THE CITY CLUB OF CLEVELAND

In September 1916, surging membership forced the City Club to move to larger quarters on the third floor of a new thirteen-story addition to the Hollenden Hotel. Occupying 8,300 square feet, the new clubrooms included a large dining room overlooking the corner of East 6th Street and Vincent Avenue, a couple of smaller dining rooms, a library (designated as a "delivery station" of the Cleveland Public Library, allowing club members to order and borrow books), a lounge, and a game room with equipment for pool and billiards. Whenever a popular speaker caused attendance to exceed the dining room's capacity of 150, the forum program could be moved either to the hotel's assembly hall or to the even larger new banquet hall, reached by the club's own stairway. The Hollenden provided the club's meals at a modest cost; by arrangement with the hotel there was no tipping.

At the Hollenden, the City Club honed its traditions and its bedrock principles of free and fair speech. In 1916, before leaving Cleveland to serve as secretary to the newly appointed Secretary of War Newton D. Baker, Ralph A. Hayes, the club's first paid secretary, penned the creed of the City Club (see frontispiece), which begins:

> I hail and harbor and hear men of every belief and party; for within my portals prejudice grows less and bias dwindles.
> I have a forum—as wholly uncensored as it is rigidly impartial. "Freedom of Speech" is graven above my rostrum; and beside it, "Fairness of Speech."

The club would be nonpartisan and democratic (with a small *d*), and it would accord a respectful hearing to speakers of every shade of political belief.

Under Francis T. "Pat" Hayes, the genial Irishman who presided as club secretary from 1916 until 1923, the City Club grew to two thousand members with a long waiting list. In addition to its regular Saturday forums, the club hosted an annual "roundup," or picnic, for members' families in the Cleveland countryside, citywide chess and checkers tournaments, and the annual Anvil Revue, which poked fun at political bigwigs and stuffed shirts. But the "heart" of the City Club, as Thomas Campbell observed in his history, was the dining room, down the center of which ran a long table known as the "trench." Around this table gathered the city's judges, lawyers, newspapermen, and others who dissected and debated current events in lively fashion.

As might be expected in a club having a large and diverse membership, luncheon table cliques developed. Administrators from the nearby board of education gravitated to what came to be called the Schoolmasters' Table. At another, over which Judge Carl Friebolin presided, sat those who enjoyed spinning the plots and puns of the club's Anvil Revue. But the most famous—some would say notorious—was the Soviet Table, which hosted the club's often noisy iconoclasts. The Soviet Table formed in the tumultuous years following World War I and the Russian Revolution. Its left-leaning habitués—the sharp-tongued Peter Witt, joined

The liberal and outspoken Peter Witt, a regular at the Soviet Table, served as commissioner of street railways under Mayor Newton D. Baker (1912–1916) and, later, two terms on Cleveland city council. THE CLEVELAND PRESS COLLECTION, MICHAEL SCHWARTZ LIBRARY, CLEVELAND STATE UNIVERSITY

Jack Raper, 1923. A humorist and columnist at the *Cleveland Press*, Raper was a fixture at the Soviet Table and regularly addressed the City Club Forum. THE CLEVELAND PRESS COLLECTION, MICHAEL SCHWARTZ LIBRARY, CLEVELAND STATE UNIVERSITY

by friends Ed Doty, Ed Byers, and John W. "Jack" Raper, a columnist for the *Cleveland Press*—didn't hesitate to criticize political leaders or their grandiose plans and projects. Club Secretary Pat Hayes gave the group its name one day, shortly after the war, when he placed a bouquet of red roses on the table and remarked, "At last your true colors! This is the Soviet Table." "None of us knew just what a Soviet was," Jack Raper would later write, "but we knew we had been called a terribly bad name. That pleased us. And we sort o' stuck it onto ourselves, like a lot of bad boys."[5]

The Sanhedrin, the club's other notable luncheon table, came into being when some regulars at the Soviet Table seceded owing to its high decibel level. Named after the supreme Jewish council in ancient Jerusalem, this quieter, more moderate coterie was led by Louis E. Siegelstein, a Romanian-born physician and surgeon, and Sidney Rosenbaum, an insurance executive. Other members included James G. Monnett Jr., the real estate editor of the *Plain Dealer;* Frank C. Cain, the mayor of Cleveland Heights; David Gibson, publisher of the *Lorain Journal;* William A. Stinchcomb, director of the Cleveland Metropolitan Park District; and lawyer Thomas J. Herbert, a future governor of Ohio. The colorful doings of the luncheon table groups usually stayed within the club, but not always. In March 1932,

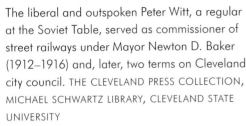

**The most famous luncheon table clique —some would say notorious—was the Soviet Table, which hosted the club's noisy iconoclasts.**

5. John W. Raper, *The Soviet Table, or the Rise of Civilization in Cleveland,* an address delivered before the City Club of Cleveland and published by the Public Affairs Committee of Cuyahoga County, 1935, 4–5.

Page one, *The City,* of September 27, 1922. Published weekly (except July and August) beginning in 1915, *The City* carried news of the City Club's upcoming events and sprightly comment about members and their doings. THE CITY CLUB OF CLEVELAND

> **During its salad days at the Hollenden, from 1916 until 1929, the City Club hosted debates on temperance, women's suffrage, birth control, city-county consolidation, and movie censorship.**

the *Plain Dealer* carried an account of a dinner at the City Club enjoyed by some two dozen members of the Sanhedrin Table, who donned skull caps for the occasion and dined by the light of a menorah. "Last night [Sanhedrin] members met at the club to eat a large meal and insult each other for a few hours . . . It was a very successful meeting," the paper deadpanned.

The spirited, fraternal fun that characterized the luncheon table groups extended to the annual City Club elections. On "Candidates' Night" (sometimes called "Candidates' Field Day"), candidates for the board of directors, together with their "campaign managers," were each allotted five minutes to present their "platforms." A toastmaster presided. Replete with costumes and props, the tradition would persist into the 1970s. A newspaper account of the 1919 contest illustrates the nature of this annual event. Cleveland school board member Mark L. Thomsen highlighted, as a credential of his candidate, W. G. Leutner, the fact that "He is not a lawyer. That's his first qualification." In his skit, *Cleveland Press* columnist Jack Raper underscored his fitness for office by "firing" his campaign manager, Carl Friebolin. Then, invoking the great statesman (President Roosevelt) "who shook this country" with his Square Deal, Raper stood up for "a Square Meal," promising City Club members soup thick enough to float a cracker and "2¾ percent hash" instead of the usual "99 percent crumbs and potatoes."

During its salad days at the Hollenden, from 1916 until 1929, the City Club hosted debates on temperance, women's suffrage, birth control, city-county consolidation, and movie censorship. It presented an astonishing roster of speakers, including Tomáš Garrigue Masaryk, who would become the principal founder of the new nation of Czechoslovakia; Jane Addams, the pioneer settlement worker and founder of Chicago's Hull House; Samuel Gompers, president of the American Federation of Labor; and the composer John Philip Sousa—the March King—who, following his talk, directed a performance by the forty-piece Glenville High School girls' band. The club hosted Éamon de Valera, leader of Ireland's struggle for independence; Syngman Rhee, who would become the first president of South Korea; and, in 1920, Franklin D. Roosevelt, a candidate for vice president of the United States.

On February 15, 1929, City Club members filled the Hollenden's banquet hall to hear an address by Ohio Attorney General Edward C. Turner.
THE CLEVELAND PRESS COLLECTION, MICHAEL SCHWARTZ LIBRARY, CLEVELAND STATE UNIVERSITY

Also appearing were the New York drama critics Heywood Broun and Robert Benchley; Clarence Darrow, defense attorney in the Scopes "Monkey" Trial; and Floyd Bennett, the aviator who only months earlier piloted Richard E. Byrd on his attempt to reach the North Pole. In 1925, Lieutenant Jack Harding, co-pilot of the first aerial circumnavigation of the world, together with Lowell Thomas, the trip's official historian, shared the story of their feat in a special evening presentation at Engineers Auditorium. The writer, historian, and philosopher Will Durant addressed the club in 1927; the African American orator, educator, and journalist William Pickens spoke in 1928; and in 1929 the club hosted Roscoe Pound, dean of Harvard Law School and author of the landmark survey of the administration of criminal justice in Cleveland, and Ida M. Tarbell, the biographer of Abraham Lincoln who had made her name with an exposé of the predatory practices of Standard Oil. Sprinkled in with such heavyweights were humorists, actors, musicians, and, of course, state and local political figures.

City Club members possessing oratorical gifts sometimes appeared at the podium. Jack Raper, who wrote the "Most Anything" column in the *Cleveland Press*, and Abba Hillel Silver, rabbi of Temple Tifereth Israel (The Temple) from 1917 until 1963, regularly addressed the club. In 1920, in

> **In January 1923, in a city whose large population of low-wage immigrant workers had embraced the message of socialism, the City Club's commitment to free speech was tested—and found wanting.**

an ambitious attempt to bring its programming to other parts of the city, the City Club established a forum extension committee under the leadership of Dudley S. Blossom, which conducted a series of public forums at the Goodrich Social Settlement, East Technical High School, and, during the summer months, in Public Square. Though short-lived, the experiment allowed club Secretary Pat Hayes to boast that the City Club that year had hosted a remarkable 46 forums with a total attendance of 30,925. Beginning in 1928, the club's reach extended even further when WHK, the city's pioneer radio station, began regular live broadcasts of the City Club Forum.

In January 1923, in a city whose large population of low-wage immigrant workers had embraced the message of socialism, the City Club's commitment to free speech was tested—and found wanting. Five years earlier, in June 1918, the Socialist Party leader Eugene V. Debs had made a speech in Canton, Ohio, opposing the World War and urging resistance to the military draft. Following the speech he was arrested in Cleveland, convicted of violating the Espionage Act, and sentenced to ten years in an Atlanta prison. Owing to Debs's declining health, President Warren G. Harding commuted his sentence to time served, effective Christmas Day 1921.

In 1922, Jack Raper, Peter Witt, and others proposed that Debs be invited to address the City Club and in December that year the public affairs committee voted to issue the invitation. City Club President Frank Cain directed that the invitation be held up until the board of directors could pass on it. On January 9, 1923, the board voted 6 to 4 in favor of extending the invitation. Club Secretary Pat Hayes issued the invitation, which Debs promptly accepted, agreeing to address the group in the near future.

Meanwhile, according to the *Plain Dealer*, "five men prominent in the business and professional life of Cleveland," indignant that Debs had been invited to speak, resigned from the City Club. Others protested by letter, and one, A. M. Goldsmith, circulated a petition calling on the board

of directors to reconsider its decision upholding the public affairs committee's decision to invite Debs. City Club President Cain refused to preside at the Debs forum "because of his personal feeling that Debs should not have been invited." When Debs learned of the dissension within the club, he gently begged off, writing to club Secretary Hayes: "Feeling disinclined . . . to obtrude where there is any question of my being welcome, or as to the right of being heard in a forum avowedly open to free speech, I beg to withdraw my acceptance and to respectfully decline the invitation of the club."[6]

This shameful incident stands alone in the annals of the City Club. If it suggested that the club needed its bedrock principle of free speech refreshed, an inspiring lesson came only a few years later. In 1929, in his dissenting opinion in *United States v. Schwimmer*, Associate Justice of the Supreme Court Oliver Wendell Holmes Jr. wrote: "If there is any principle of the Constitution that more imperatively calls for attachment than any other, it is the principle of free thought—not free thought for those who agree with us but freedom for the thought that we hate." The City Club of Cleveland would be further tested during its first century, but it would never again flinch as it had in 1923.

## A home of its own

Cleveland in 1929 was riding high. It was an industrial and economic colossus whose residents could look with pride at municipal progress and advancement in the arts, medicine, education, and city beautification. Tall office buildings had transformed the skyline, the city's handsome Group Plan of public buildings had garnered national attention, and the Cleveland Union Terminal on Public Square—a "city within a city" with its interconnected railroad station, office buildings, hotel, and department store—was nearing completion.

As a heady and prosperous decade drew to a close, the City Club made plans to move yet again, this time to the north portion of the Childs Building at 712 Vincent Avenue, a stone's throw from its quarters in the Hollenden, on which

6. On June 10, 1923, before an audience of seven thousand union members in Cleveland's Public Hall, an unrepentant Debs "finished" his Canton speech. "It was here in [Cleveland]," Debs said, "that I was indicted and tried in a capitalistic court, and of course convicted. Had they been wise enough to leave that speech alone, it never would have been heard of outside of Canton.

As it is, it has been translated into twelve languages and spread around the world." Debs assailed President Woodrow Wilson, whose campaign slogan in 1916 had been "He kept us out of war." Of the Canton speech, Debs said, "There is not one word I would retract. There is not one word I would apologize for. There is not one word I would take back if it carried me to the gallows."

The City Club, 1937. The club occupied the middle of a block-long street known as "Short Vincent." Connecting East Sixth and East Ninth Streets, it was the setting for stately banks, restaurants, offices, and, with the end of Prohibition, such nightspots as the Roxy Burlesque and the Theatrical Grill. CLEVELAND PUBLIC LIBRARY PHOTOGRAPH COLLECTION

it secured a long-term lease. The newly remodeled clubhouse would be financed by issuing stock to club members and by voluntary contributions. Almost one-third of the club's total cost of $45,000 would come from Childs restaurant, which would provide food service in the new club. As a parting gesture, the Hollenden presented the Sanhedrin luncheon group with its large round table. Not to be outdone, members of the Soviet Table purchased their own round table and presented it to the City Club. Large enough to seat twenty, it bore, at the center, a carved hammer and sickle within a red star, flanked by black bulls, the symbol Jack Raper employed in his *Cleveland Press* column whenever he found it necessary to challenge a politician's veracity. Around these decorations were carved the names of the table's donors.

The new clubhouse was dedicated at a members-only luncheon on Tuesday, November 12, 1929. Designed by Cleveland architects Paul Ockert and George W. Teare, the new City Club was simple and comfortable. The exterior— "vaguely English, with a touch of the modern," as the dedication booklet described it—was distinguished by a façade of Indiana limestone and tall leaded-glass windows. In the center bay, carved wood panels separating the first and second stories featured, in relief, Moses Cleaveland, the city's founder, flanked by male figures said to represent "a cross section of the community as typified in City Club membership." Inside, the club was extensively paneled in knotty pine, its décor said to mix "early American with the modern." A high-ceilinged dining room and the kitchen occupied the ground floor; a mezzanine contained coat-check

rooms and toilet facilities; and on the second floor were offices, a large lounge with fireplace, and a billiard room. With its new clubhouse, the dedication booklet declared, the City Club "stands now upon the threshold of a new era which promises much toward future success, vigor and usefulness."

In fact, the City Club stood at a precipice. Black Tuesday, the most devastating stock market crash in the history of the United States, had occurred only two weeks earlier, signaling the start of an economic downturn that would bring Cleveland, and the nation, to its knees. The City Club would carry on, but, as Tom Campbell later wrote, "Only those most deeply committed to the club's ideals continued to give their time and money." That it survived at all was in large measure due to Jack Lafferty. Lafferty, a former insurance and automobile salesman appointed City Club secretary in 1931, worked hard to put the club back on its feet and would serve as club secretary until 1957. To Lafferty's name must be added that of Hilda Snyder. Hired as a bookkeeper in 1929, Snyder did anything that needed doing, even working without pay during the Depression, according to her obituary. Promoted to assistant secretary in 1944, Snyder would serve the club for nearly fifty years.

As an economic pall settled over Cleveland, the City Club continued with its core activities: congenial and sometimes raucous luncheons, weekly forums (except in summer), Candidates' Night, and the annual Anvil Revue. However, with diminished financial resources, the club hosted fewer out-of-town speakers and instead, to save on travel expenses, filled its forum calendar with talks by government officials, college presidents and professors, and, not infrequently, the City Club's own members. Peter Witt, Jack Raper, and Rabbi Abba Hillel Silver regularly appeared at the podium. A local weather forecaster spoke on the "whimsicalities" of the weather, a transmission engineer with the Ohio Bell Telephone Company on developments in communications. Still, some nationally known figures continued to pepper the forum schedule. Club members heard talks by the psychiatrist Dr. Karl Menninger; journalists Lincoln Steffens and Drew Pearson; George Gallup, a pioneer in scientific polling techniques; and NAACP Secretary William Pickens.

As President Franklin D. Roosevelt put in place an array of programs focused on relief for the unemployed, recovery of the economy to normal levels, and reform of the financial system to prevent a repeat depression, proponents of the New Deal, including the U.S. secretary of commerce and representatives of the National Recovery Act and the Work Projects Administration, appeared before the City Club. In 1933, Representative Henry B. Steagall, Republican of Alabama, addressed the club. That year Steagall co-sponsored the Glass-Steagall Act, which introduced critical banking reforms and established the Federal Deposit Insurance Corporation. Critics of the New Deal were also invited to speak, including James F. Lincoln, president of Cleveland's Lincoln Electric Company ("Do We Want the New Deal or Prosperity?").

Opposite page: From 1929 until 1971, the City Club occupied its own two-story clubhouse at 712 Vincent Avenue, a block-long street known as "Short Vincent." THE WESTERN RESERVE HISTORICAL SOCIETY

John J. "Jack" Lafferty (1892–1970), shown here in 1933, served as secretary of the City Club from 1931 until 1957. An astute manager, he helped the club weather the Great Depression and the Second World War. THE CLEVELAND PRESS COLLECTION, MICHAEL SCHWARTZ LIBRARY, CLEVELAND STATE UNIVERSITY

# CLEVELAND'S ARISTOPHANES

## Carl Friebolin and the City Club's Anvil Revue

"It matters not whether you are a Republican, a Democrat, a Progressive or a mugwump," read the invitation to a "smoker" at the City Club in January 1914. Cyrus Locher, Daniel E. Morgan, and Carl D. Friebolin furnished the evening's entertainment, consisting of good-natured roasts, songs, and nonsense. Stunt Nite, as it came to be called, became an annual event at the new club "formed for the purpose of investigation, discussion and improvement of civic conditions and affairs in Cleveland."

After complaining about the "lousy" lines he was given, Carl Friebolin (1878–1967) was prevailed upon to take complete responsibility for writing the show. Friebolin, a former state legislator and protégé of Mayor

Tom L. Johnson, was appointed by President Woodrow Wilson as a United States referee in bankruptcy for the northern Ohio district in 1916; he would remain in that position for the remainder of his career.

Of his early efforts, Friebolin would later recall, "I wrote the lyrics, the script, everything. I directed [too] and if a song was coming I had to beat it around behind the curtain and play the piano." Beginning in 1921, Joseph S. "Joe" Newman, head of the Newman-Stern Company and a talented punster, joined Friebolin to write the show's lyrics.

Stunt Nite quickly evolved from a collection of musical-comedy skits into fully staged productions complete with costumes, scenery, and music, held in various downtown theaters. The annual shows were open only to City Club members, with compli-

Curtain call, May 1958. With impartiality and razor-edge wit, playwright Carl Friebolin, left, and lyricist Joe Newman, the longtime creators of the City Club's Anvil Revue, punctured

political pretension wherever it was to be found.
THE CLEVELAND PRESS COLLECTION, MICHAEL SCHWARTZ LIBRARY, CLEVELAND STATE UNIVERSITY

Leo Boylan, Pete DiLeone, Karl Driggs, and Jim Rigelhaupt (left to right) starred in the 1939 production *Sauce for the Goose Step, or Debt Takes a Holiday.* THE WESTERN RESERVE HISTORICAL SOCIETY

Programs for Anvil Revue productions were often professionally designed, such as this one by the artist John Duncan for the 1945 show. THE WESTERN RESERVE HISTORICAL SOCIETY

mentary box seats reserved for the "goats"— the political, civic, and business leaders who were being lampooned. The first full-blown play, presented in 1917 at the 1,400-seat Metropolitan Theater, was *Fitness and Fury, or the Follibilities of the City Manager,* in which Friebolin garnered laughs by depicting a future Cleveland on the day after the adoption of the city manager plan—a form of government then being hotly debated, especially within the City Club, by good-government advocates and staunch defenders of the elected mayor and ward system.

In 1924, after Cleveland had implemented the city manager plan, Friebolin wrote a biting sendup titled *The Maurice Plan, or Burning the Scandal at Both Ends,* roasting Maurice Maschke, county Republican leader, for his backroom deal making.

Also on the program: the "Standard Oil quartet" singing "Pack Up the Boodle in the Old Hand Bag"; and street railway Commissioner Peter Witt, an acolyte of Cleveland's progressive Mayor Tom L. Johnson (who famously argued for municipal ownership of public utilities), pleading for "municipal ownership of the city hall." Friebolin's offering in 1932, after Cleveland voters rescinded the city manager plan, was titled *The Plan Handlers, or After Election Comes Mourning.*

In 1926, the annual City Club production was renamed the Anvil Revue. In 1931, the show moved to the new 2,600-seat Music Hall in Public Auditorium, where it was staged each spring, usually in April. Thenceforth, the City Club production was opened to the public and became a rite of

Anvil Revue cast members were necessarily versatile, playing both male and female roles until 1966, when women joined the cast. In the 1955 production, they danced the cancan in a skit referencing the 2nd Pan American Games, held in Mexico. THE CLEVELAND PRESS COLLECTION, MICHAEL SCHWARTZ LIBRARY, CLEVELAND STATE UNIVERSITY

spring. By the 1940s, the Anvil Revue was playing to capacity houses, typically offering two performances: a Saturday matinee for women and a Saturday evening production for men, including a large complement of public officials. Beginning in 1961, women —to Friebolin's chagrin—were permitted to attend any performance.

For almost five decades, Friebolin skillfully and hilariously skewered a procession of councilmen, mayors, city managers, governors, congressmen, senators, presidents, business tycoons, and assorted muckety-

mucks, who felt the barbs of his sharp but never cruel wit. At curtain time, he would appear on stage to make his customary declaration that the presentation was "in the spirit of the traditional American disrespect for authority"; at the same time, he would announce, disingenuously, that this "is positively my last show."

Friebolin's 46th and final show, in 1963, was titled *Play, Fidel, Play, or Stop the Press, I Want to Get Off*. Previewing the show, *Cleveland Plain Dealer* theater critic Peter Bellamy called it "one of the funniest of Anvil Revues, and I have seen some 30 . . . Judge Friebolin's dialogue is devastating." Bellamy credited other longtime contributors, including Walter H. Belding for musical arrangements; Barclay Leathem, professor of drama at Western Reserve University, as director; Eleanor Frampton, choreographer; and Nathan A. Schwartz, stage manager. He also cited Harold Glickman for his 25th annual portrayal of Ben Sapp, citizen and taxpayer. A photograph of Friebolin accompanying the article was captioned "Cleveland's Aristophanes," alluding to the comic playwright of ancient Athens.

In 1964, one thousand persons attended a testimonial dinner at the Hotel Sheraton-Cleveland honoring the 86-year-old Friebolin. U.S. Senators Frank J. Lausche and Stephen M. Young were there. So was Mayor Ralph S. Locher, who told him, "Cleveland, sir, has been the better for your presence." After letting loose with a few barbs and accepting the gift of a contoured chair especially made to fit his diminutive frame, Friebolin and his admirers watched an abbreviated production titled "This Is the Show That Wasn't."

The Anvil Revue continued for a few more years, carried by the talents of Peter DiLeone, Fred Stashower, and other members of the then all-male club. Women joined the cast in 1966 (until then, female roles had been played by men). But without Friebolin and Newman, who had died in 1960, it was never the same. In 1976, the City Club abandoned the annual show. "We've had increasing trouble for several years in whipping up interest," Alan J. Davis, executive director of the City Club, told the *Cleveland Press* that year. "Perhaps it has just outlived its time."

In 1979, the Anvil Revue was revived as a radio program, produced and largely written by Robert Conrad, president of WCLV-FM. The radio version of the show (which was often presented as a program of the City Club Forum) lasted until 2002, when it, too, ran out of steam.

Jack Bialosky, playing the White Rabbit, gives a lift to the perennial character Ben Sapp, the beleaguered citizen and taxpayer played by Harold J. Glickman, in the 1961 Anvil Revue, *That New Jack Magic, or Bennie in Blunderland.*
THE WESTERN RESERVE HISTORICAL SOCIETY

The Soviet Table, date unknown, was a haven for the City Club's iconoclasts. In 1935, the printer and City Club member William Feather, in his self-published magazine, criticized the "malcontents" of the Soviet Table for impeding civic progress. His tirade against "the anti-everything boys" prompted Jack Raper, a regular at the table and a columnist at the *Cleveland Press,* to reply in a speech at the City Club Forum on February 23, 1935. Later published as a pamphlet, *The Soviet Table, or the Rise of Civilization* provides a remarkable window into local politics of the period. THE WESTERN RESERVE HISTORICAL SOCIETY

During the 1930s, the City Club further solidified its standing as *the* city institution where candidates for office presented their credentials and debated their opponents, and where local issues received a thorough airing. Among those issues was Cleveland's eight-year experiment, begun in 1923, with the city manager plan of government, a favorite target of the Soviet Table. Attorney Saul S. Danaceau, a Soviet Table regular, authored a charter amendment to abolish the manager plan that would appear on the ballot in November 1931. Prior to the vote, in a speech to the City Club, William R. Hopkins, a former Republican city manager running for the city council as an independent, broke his silence about his years in office. Hopkins attacked the Republican political boss Maurice Maschke, charging that the whole of city government was run for the private profit of Maschke and a few others at the helm of the Republican Party. If anyone wanted to know how the "Maschke system" works, Hopkins said, let him ask any contractor doing business with the city, any city employee under civil service protection, any policeman working the vice and gambling districts, or any salesman of equipment purchased by the city. The speech was front-page news in Cleveland and was even reported by the *New York Times* under the headline "Cleveland Learns about Its Politics." Accepting an invitation to reply the following week, Maschke branded Hopkins a "poseur" and a "hypocrite" in front of a record-breaking audience in the Hollenden ballroom. A week later, voters approved the charter amendment, returning Cleveland to the mayor-council form of government.

As the Depression took its toll on Cleveland's fabric and psyche, and some began to ponder the city's evident decline, the City Club presented a panel discussion addressing the question "What Is Right and/or Wrong with Cleveland?" Following the Great Lakes Exposition, which temporarily lifted the city's spirits over the summers of 1936 and 1937, the club gathered another panel of experts to consider the perennial problem of lakefront planning. And, in 1938, in a city still jittery over the unsolved Torso Murders, Safety Director Eliot Ness assured the City Club audience that the reorganization of the police department, including the introduction of radio-equipped police cars, was well under way.

Whether in anticipation of its silver anniversary or to boost its sagging membership rolls, in 1936 the club published an illustrated pamphlet titled *The City Club . . . a Civilized Idea*. Photographs showed off its large and comfortable lounge and the dining room with its "famous" tables that provided "daily excitement." Free speech, wrote the unnamed author, "has worn out the carpet in the dining room where hundreds of members of the Club assemble during each week to argue and listen; and at the Saturday forums to hear the great and the near great champion every shade of opinion and belief." The pamphlet advised prospective members that the club had established a graduated scale of fees and dues "in order that no one otherwise eligible may be denied membership because of cost." Quarterly dues ranged from $6.25 for "seniors" (35 years of age and over) down to $1.50 for students 18 years of age and over. Membership required the signatures of two "proposers," or sponsors.

On Saturday, December 4, 1937, the City Club marked its 25th anniversary quietly with a luncheon and speeches by Daniel Morgan, the first president of the club, and Mayo Fesler, secretary of the Cleveland Civic League and a founder of the club. The following week, at the annual Candidates' Night, nearly five hundred City Club members

Candidates' Night at the City Club, 1937. At this annual event, club members vying for election to the board of directors, together with their campaign "managers," put on humorous skits to garner votes, a process the *Cleveland Plain Dealer* called "a combination mock political convention and burlesque show." THE WESTERN RESERVE HISTORICAL SOCIETY

An unnamed luncheon table group at the City Club, 1932, consisted "mostly of young men who have been associated with the foreign affairs group [of] the Adult Education Association," according to the accompanying article in the *Cleveland Press*, whose "chatter runs to brainy stuff." The photograph is notable as the earliest to include an African American. THE CLEVELAND PRESS COLLECTION, MICHAEL SCHWARTZ LIBRARY, CLEVELAND STATE UNIVERSITY

7. Christopher G. Wye, "Midwest Ghetto: Patterns of Negro Life and Thought in Cleveland, Ohio, 1929–1945" (PhD diss., Kent State University, 1973), 465, 469.

gathered to enjoy skits put on by eight candidates, each with his "campaign manager," vying for four seats on the board. The next day's *Plain Dealer* provided an account of the revelry, which saw the "acidulous" (and ultra-liberal) Jack Raper managing the campaign of former Congressman Chester C. Bolton, a staunch Republican. "Politics does indeed make for strange bedfellows," read the caption of a photograph showing the pair in action. Another photograph showed the tightly packed crowd—all white, it should be noted—each man nattier than the next in suit and tie, not a few chomping cigars as they signaled, amid great hilarity, thumbs up or down on a candidate's performance.

Such occasions surely provided club members a welcome respite from economic woes even as they demonstrated the warm embrace to be found within the City Club no matter one's position on the political spectrum. While that warm embrace presumably would have been extended to any Cleveland man having the time, means, and requisite sponsors, there is no evidence of African American members during the City Club's first two decades. Although the Great Migration of southern blacks during and after the First World War had seen the city's African American population increase from (in round numbers) 8,000 in 1910 to 34,000 in 1920 and to 72,000 by 1930, African Americans held few professional jobs compared with whites, according to one scholar.[7]

The first African American member of the City Club who can be documented is George Brown, an examiner with the Cleveland Civil Service Commission, who appears in a photograph of a City Club luncheon table group having a special interest in foreign affairs published by the *Cleveland Press* in 1932. A 1938 *Cleveland Plain Dealer* profile of William Randall Conners, executive secretary of the Negro Welfare Association (later renamed the Urban League of Cleveland), noted his membership in the City Club; another article the same year reported a testimonial banquet in his honor at the City Club hosted by Assistant City Prosecutor Norman S. Minor (after whom Cleveland's African American bar association would be named when it was organized in 1980), an event also reported in the club's newsletter, *The City*. In 1960, William T. "Bill" McKnight, an assistant city law director, would become the first African American elected as a director of the City Club, but the number of black members remained small well into the 1970s.

From its inception, the City Club enjoyed a symbiotic relationship with the local press. Editors and reporters for Cleveland's major dailies were often members of the club; they served on its board, reported on its activities, and wrote flattering articles and editorials. In 1940, City Club President Philip W. Porter, news editor of the *Plain Dealer*, together with John W. Barkley, initiated an effort to establish a foundation to support the club's weekly forums. The City Club Forum Foundation, the *Plain Dealer* reported, would "permit non-members, women and radio listeners as well as active club members to support [the club's] widely-known Saturday forums . . . It is hoped that enough large gifts ultimately will be made to provide an endowment fund, interest from which would pay the forum's operating expense, which until now has been borne entirely by the club." Indeed, the newspaper asserted, with the advent of radio broadcasts in the late twenties, the City Club Forum had grown to become an "educational institution," with a listening audience across northern Ohio estimated to number between 75,000 and 100,000.

In addition to club partisans Carl Friebolin, Daniel Morgan, and Peter Witt, the incorporators of the City Club Forum Foundation included a newspaper troika: Paul Bellamy, editor of the *Cleveland Plain Dealer*, Louis B. Seltzer, editor of the *Cleveland Press*, and Nathaniel R. Howard, editor of the *Cleveland News*. Friebolin, the first president of the foundation, made the first gift, and at the opening forum of the 1940–41 season, City Club President Philip Porter announced a gift of $1,000 from Congresswoman Frances P. Bolton in memory of her late husband, Congressman Chester C. Bolton, a director of the City Club at the time of his death. Although its funds grew slowly—the next large gift, $1,000 from the Cleveland Foundation, did not come until 1946—the foundation, it

**With the advent of radio broadcasts in the late twenties, the City Club Forum had grown to become an "educational institution," with a listening audience across northern Ohio estimated to number between 75,000 and 100,000.**

At the Christmas luncheon on Saturday, December 21, 1940, City Club President Philip W. Porter, news editor of the *Cleveland Plain Dealer*, passed the gavel to his successor, Nathaniel R. Howard, editor of the *Cleveland News*. CLEVELAND PUBLIC LIBRARY PHOTOGRAPH COLLECTION

was hoped, would ensure the future of the City Club Forum, which had evolved to become a civic institution separate and apart from the men's social club out of which it had sprung.

On Saturday, October 10, 1942, the artist and writer Rockwell Kent opened a new season of the City Club Forum. Women were invited to attend the special program, at which the club dedicated a new mural filling the rear wall of the dining room. On behalf of a committee of donors, Appellate Judge Daniel E. Morgan presented the mural, executed by the social-realist painter Elmer W. Brown.[8] Titled *Freedom of Speech*, it depicted Magna Carta, Lady Justice holding her scales, the Bill of Rights, the printing press, and other symbols said to represent the ideals of the City Club.

In the years leading up to America's entry into World War II, the City Club Forum increasingly focused on global issues, featuring authors and journalists who presented their insights on events in Europe and Asia. In the spring of 1940, Melvin K. Whiteleather, an Associated Press correspondent just back from Germany, made front-page news when he presented "A Six-Year Close-Up of Hitler" to an overflow audience; the "lifeblood of the [German] nation," he told the City Club, had been "poured into the German Army." Later that year, James R. Young, a foreign correspondent for the International News Service, presented an insider's look at Japan's invasion of China and warned of its designs on the Dutch East Indies. Following the attack on Pearl Harbor, the City Club hosted a steady lineup of historians and journalists discussing myriad aspects of the war and the progress of Allied forces. In 1944, in the midst of war, the sociologist, historian, and civil-rights activist W. E. B. Du Bois returned to the City Club, where he delivered a forceful address in which he assailed the color line in the armed forces, calling it "one of the most flagrant denials of everything we are supposed to be fighting for." Du Bois's talk left club members peppering him with questions long after the forum ended and continued until the speaker finally had to break away to catch his train.

> In 1944, W. E. B. Du Bois returned to the City Club, where he assailed the color line in the armed forces, calling it "one of the most flagrant denials of everything we are supposed to be fighting for."

## Racial disparity and a declining city

At war's end, global politics, especially the looming Soviet threat, claimed a central place in City Club programming. Forum speakers also addressed emerging technologies such as electronics, atomic energy, automation, and advances in medical research, while debates featuring state and local political candidates and issues filled the calendar each October. Four days after Democratic President Harry S. Truman's upset victory over Republican Thomas E. Dewey in the 1948 presidential election, James B. Reston, a correspondent for the *New York Times*, was at the podium to deliver a postmortem. The press, he admitted, had got it wrong. "We were too isolated with other reporters, just as Dewey was too isolated with politicians. We overlooked the people."

8. Elmer W. Brown (1909–1971), an African American, studied at the Cleveland School of Art and taught at Cleveland's Karamu House. Through the Public Works of Art Project, he also executed murals at the Valley View public housing project. Brown later worked as an artist for Cleveland's American Greetings Corporation.

At the City Club Forum of October 12, 1946, a capacity audience listened attentively as David Dietz, science editor of the *Cleveland Press,* described "The Future of Atomic Energy." THE CLEVELAND PRESS COLLECTION, MICHAEL SCHWARTZ LIBRARY, CLEVELAND STATE UNIVERSITY

It was a sentimental gathering on Saturday, October 11, 1952, when the City Club marked its 40th anniversary. At the podium was Ralph Hayes, the club's first paid secretary and the author of the City Club creed. Hayes had left Cleveland in 1916 and gone on to a long career as an executive with Coca-Cola in New York. In the dining room were many of the club's surviving charter members and former presidents. Introducing the speaker, Carl Friebolin said that Hayes had "mothered the club" in its first years. Hayes returned the compliment, declaring that the City Club of Cleveland "may well have created . . . the finest and freest forum in the United States." Hayes remarked on the astonishing trajectory of the club: born under President Taft, it had successively witnessed the economic boom of the 1920s, a disastrous depression, and two world wars. "While this club was growing up, this country, too, was being thrust into a position rarely paralleled in history," he said. At the conclusion of his remarks, Hayes wryly noted, "This forum didn't invent free speech . . . But we have done this much for it: we've exercised it till the cows come home!"

As the city's thriving wartime and postwar industries lifted Cleveland out of the Depression, Jack Lafferty was still at the helm as club secretary—he would not retire until 1957—having mastered the art of steering a middle course.

> **"While this club was growing up, this country, too, was being thrust into a position rarely paralleled in history."**
> **—Ralph Hayes**

City Club Secretary Jack Lafferty, center, shares a celebratory moment with the club's newly elected president, Dr. Ralph E. Crow, at left, and George B. Mayer, vice president, 1955. CLEVELAND PUBLIC LIBRARY PHOTOGRAPH COLLECTION

"My Republican friends think of me as a New Dealer; my Democratic friends consider me a rank Republican," he once quipped. Forum speakers of note during the 1950s ranged from baseball commissioner Ford Frick to the writer Vance Packard, whose best-selling book, *The Hidden Persuaders*, probed the dark intersection of advertising and consumption, to Farid Zeineddine, the Syrian ambassador to the United States, who described a postwar Arab world in turmoil. In 1953, amid rising fear of communism intensified by the Korean War, Rabbi Abba Hillel Silver delivered a stirring address on "America's Stake in Human Freedom" that earned repeated standing ovations from a large City Club audience. The liberal religious leader warned against "a global armament race which will impoverish the peoples of the earth— ourselves included." Alluding to "certain congressional investigating committees," he warned against demagogues— surely a reference to Senator Joseph McCarthy—telling the City Club: "In fighting communism, we must be doubly sure we are fighting Communists, not others whose views we do not happen to like."

As City Club presidents continued to bring the forum to order each Saturday at one o'clock, some speakers began to press the issue of social justice at home. In 1945, the Reverend Wade H. McKinney, the longtime pastor of Cleveland's Antioch Baptist Church and a respected voice of the African American community, had told the City Club about deleterious conditions in the city's Central Avenue neighborhood, where 90,000 of the city's 100,000 Negroes lived, asserting that under its "ghetto housing setup," Cleveland "can never have a wholesome race relationship in its schools or in its civic life." When McKinney returned to the City Club podium in 1958, vast areas of the Central Avenue community were being bulldozed for urban renewal and the displaced were migrating north and east to the Hough and Glenville neighborhoods. McKinney again asserted that the problems of inadequate housing, high rents, and the exploitation of Cleveland's Negroes by white landlords who now lived in the suburbs continued unabated.

Notwithstanding heavy promotion of the slogan "The Best Location in the Nation"—coined in 1944 by the Cleveland Electric Illuminating Company to lure industrial development to Cleveland—the central city's postwar decline was obvious and troubling. In January 1959, the City Club devoted a series of three forums to the question "Is Cleveland a Dying City?" While surely well-intentioned, the programs, which failed to include even a single African American voice, elicited a biting response from William O. Walker, publisher and editor of the *Call and Post*, the city's black newspaper. In a column titled "Nobody Wants to Hear from Us," Walker wrote, "Since Negroes constitute 28 percent of the population of Cleveland, it seems strange that the City Club would ignore the views of so many people." He continued:

Conditions are like they are today, because so many Cleveland people presume to talk for the Negro, while the

Negro himself is never heard. It seems inconceivable to many Americans that the Negro should have anything to say but "yessa boss."

The Negro question is one of the most important in any American city today. Most of the ills of our urban centers are blamed on the Negro. The South blames all of its ills on the Negro . . .

It seems the more America tries to dodge the Negro question, the more places it turns up. Sooner or later this question will have to be faced here in Cleveland as well as elsewhere in the nation. And it cannot be properly and adequately faced until the Negro is heard as a part of its solution.

In an era of gray-flannel suits and suburban contentment, the City Club continued to present compelling and often provocative newsmakers. Such notables as Alan F. Guttmacher, president of Planned Parenthood; the Harvard economist John Kenneth Galbraith; and syndicated editorial cartoonist Herbert L. Block ("Herblock") appeared. The businessman-financier (and City Club member) Cyrus S. Eaton, a controversial figure owing to his advocacy of better relations with the Soviet Union, twice addressed the club during the 1950s, drawing large crowds. The urbanist Jane Jacobs, author of *The Death and Life of Great American Cities*, criticized the physical isolation of Cleveland's cultural facilities, far away from the downtown, as bad urban planning, and the investigative journalist I. F. Stone presented "Some Unflattering Resemblances between the U.S. and the U.S.S.R." James J. Kirkpatrick, editor of the *Richmond News-Leader*, made the case for states' rights; and Senator Strom Thurmond, Democrat of South Carolina, charged that the federal government was censoring anti-Communist statements out of the speeches of American military leaders because they were in conflict with U.S. foreign policy. (Thurmond's segregationist views became evident during the question-and-answer period. Asked about his voting record on civil rights, he replied [as paraphrased by the *Plain Dealer*]: "People feel more kindly toward the Negro in the South than they do in the North . . . They don't have riots in the South as they do in northern cities. Negroes have as good schools [as whites] . . . and education is a matter reserved to the states.")

In keeping with its creedal commitment to "hear men of every belief," in February 1962 the City Club hosted Robert H. W. Welch Jr., founder and president of the John Birch Society. According to a page-one story in the *Plain Dealer*, four hundred members and guests attended, with three hundred seated in the dining room and the overflow listening by loudspeaker in the upstairs lounge. After presenting a brief introduction to the organization, the proponent of anti-communism, limited government, and a "constitutional republic" submitted to a barrage of questions from the live and radio audiences. The questioners—including several African Americans, according to the *Plain Dealer*—drew

**In January 1959, the City Club devoted a series of three forums to the question "Is Cleveland a Dying City?" The programs failed to include even a single African American voice, eliciting a biting response from William O. Walker in the *Call and Post*, the city's black newspaper.**

him out on the subject of civil rights. Welch charged that the civil rights movement led by the Reverend Martin Luther King Jr. was "more closely connected with Communism than Christianity"; that the Supreme Court under Chief Justice Earl Warren had "usurped powers not given it by the Constitution" and Warren should be "impeached"; and that the chief result of the 1954 decision outlawing segregated schools "has been to stir up troubles which were not necessary at all . . ." Maintaining that the United States had inherited a republic from its founding fathers, Welch called democracy "a weapon of demagoguery and a perennial fraud."

Eighteen months later, on November 22, 1963, the abrupt loss of President John F. Kennedy to an assassin's bullet would leave the nation distraught and turn a page in its history. Dr. Frank P. Graham, a member of the U.N. Secretariat's staff, spoke at the City Club the next day, briefly prefacing his talk on "The U.N.: A Moral Imperative in an Atomic Age" with an acknowledgement of Lee Harvey Oswald's heinous act. "Poison and hate have done their worst and left us desolate," he said. "But the American people, in remembrance of President Kennedy, will rise, I believe, in a mighty resolve to carry forward . . . his devotion to fulfilling the American dream."

"STOP THE PRESSES," *Cleveland Plain Dealer* columnist Mary Hirschfield declared on March 3, 1964. "City Club directors are seriously considering moving the Saturday Forum beginning this fall, from Saturday to a midweek date . . . Reason is obvious. It's very difficult to get any kind of a crowd downtown on Saturdays," she wrote, adding, "Facing only a Corporal's guard for an audience is discouraging to speakers." Indeed, times had changed. The workweek ended on Friday, and most City Club members had long since moved to the suburbs. Beginning in October 1964, the City Club Forum shifted to Friday, with lunch served at noon and the forum starting promptly at 12:30 p.m. Beginning in 1968, another culture-driven shift occurred as the City Club gradually moved to a year-round schedule of programs.

The revamped schedule came amid growing political and racial strife across the nation. There was increasing unease over the Vietnam War, and the civil rights movement was gaining ground. In Cleveland, a gaping yet, to many, invisible racial divide became obvious in July 1966 with the Hough Riots. Lasting four days and resulting in four deaths and millions of dollars in property damage, the riots, together with the sight of National Guard troops patrolling the city's streets, shocked a complacent white population, sowing fear for the future of a city that, seemingly overnight, had come to epitomize the nation's "urban crisis." Amid heightened racial tensions, in April 1967 the City Club Forum gave a respectful hearing to George Wallace, the former governor of Alabama and a presidential aspirant then on a tour of northern cities. Protestors and supporters outside the club's curtained windows offered opposing chants as Wallace denounced "the

"STOP THE PRESSES. City Club directors are seriously considering moving the Saturday Forum beginning this fall, from Saturday to a midweek date . . . Reason is obvious. It's very difficult to get any kind of a crowd downtown on Saturdays. Facing only a Corporal's guard for an audience is discouraging to speakers." —Mary Hirschfield, *Cleveland Plain Dealer*, March 3, 1964.

liberal, left-wing media," bureaucrats, college professors, judges, and politicians. Six months later, on November 4, 1967, the City Club hosted a historic mayoral debate between Republican Seth C. Taft, the grandson of President William Howard Taft, and Democrat Carl B. Stokes, the son of a cleaning woman. Three days later, Stokes narrowly won the election, becoming the first African American to govern a major American city.

Stokes's election put Cleveland in the national spotlight and brought hope and optimism to the city's African Americans. Less than six months later, however, came the numbing nightmare of two assassinations in close succession. On April 4, 1968, a sniper shot and killed the Reverend Martin Luther King Jr. as he stood on the balcony of a motel in Memphis, Tennessee, where King had gone to express solidarity with striking sanitation workers. In his quest for the Democratic presidential nomination, Senator Robert F. Kennedy was due to visit Cleveland the next day and address a City Club audience of 1,200 at the Hotel Sheraton-Cleveland. Kennedy put aside his prepared remarks and spoke for barely ten minutes; he took no questions. "This is a time of shame and sorrow," he said. "It is not a day for politics." He continued:

> I have saved this one opportunity to speak briefly to you about this mindless menace of violence in America which again stains our land and every one of our lives . . .
>
> Why? What has violence ever accomplished? What has it ever created? No martyr's cause has ever been stilled by

**Amid heightened racial tensions, in April 1967 the City Club Forum gave a respectful hearing to former Alabama Governor George Wallace, a presidential aspirant on a tour of northern cities.**

Near the close of the historic 1967 Cleveland mayoral campaign, Carl B. Stokes (standing) debated opponent Seth Taft (seated foreground, left of center) at the City Club. Stokes would win the election, becoming the first African American mayor of a major American city. THE CLEVELAND PRESS COLLECTION, MICHAEL SCHWARTZ LIBRARY, CLEVELAND STATE UNIVERSITY

A somber Robert F. Kennedy addressed the City Club on April 5, 1968, the day after the assassination of the Reverend Martin Luther King Jr. "This is a time of shame and sorrow. It is not a day for politics," he told an audience of 1,200 at the Hotel Sheraton-Cleveland. Kennedy, who was seeking the Democratic nomination for president, was accompanied by his wife Ethel.
THE CLEVELAND PRESS COLLECTION, MICHAEL SCHWARTZ LIBRARY, CLEVELAND STATE UNIVERSITY

9. When she spoke at the City Club in 2000, Kathleen Kennedy Townsend, then serving as lieutenant governor of Maryland, would tell Executive Director Jim Foster that this was her father's most moving and, in some ways, most important speech.

his assassin's bullet. No wrongs have ever been righted by riots and civil disorders. A sniper is only a coward, not a hero; and an uncontrollable mob is only the voice of madness, not the voice of the people.[9]

Kennedy cancelled his planned rally outside the hotel, where thousands awaited him, and returned to Washington. Two months later, following his victory in the California presidential primary, Kennedy himself was felled by the "mindless menace" he had lamented. He was shot by Sirhan Sirhan, a Palestinian Arab (and a Christian), and mortally wounded. He died the next day.

In December 1969, Tom Campbell, a professor of history at Cleveland State University, was elected president of the City Club. Born in Eniskillen, Northern Ireland, where he worked as a baker before immigrating to the United States, Campbell brought a fresh vision to the post and a determination to emphasize local issues because, he told a reporter for the *Cleveland Press*, "urban problems are the great problems of our times."

Women, meanwhile, were becoming aware of "the problem that has no name" thanks to Betty Friedan's seminal manifesto, *The Feminine Mystique*, published in 1963. Three years later, Friedan, with others, founded the National

Organization for Women, which aimed to bring women into the mainstream of American society in equal partnership with men. Feminists were demanding more opportunities in the workplace and admittance to men-only institutions, including private clubs. How, in good conscience, could the City Club expect women to contribute to the support of its forums—even, on occasion, to speak at them—but deny them membership? "Next Friday," read a snarky item in Mary Hirschfield's *Plain Dealer* column of March 13, 1965, "women will be admitted to the City Club's Friday Forum if they are invited by a member. Don't miss it, gals."

In March 1969, City Club directors voted to end the ban on women guests at most forums; club membership, however, would still be limited to men only. Even this was too tradition-shattering for some. Radio talk-show host Sidney Andorn, a past president of the City Club and chairman of the club's forum committee, formed a group called SEX— standing for, he told the *Plain Dealer*, "Stop Equality on the spot (X marks the spot)"—and vowed to circulate a petition demanding a membership referendum on the question. (Nothing came of his bluster.)

Amid the nation's cultural upheaval and political and racial unrest, the City Club hosted a succession of compelling speakers. In February 1969, Dr. Benjamin Spock, the noted baby-doctor-turned-war-protester, delivered a polemic against the war in Vietnam, calling it "totally illegal and immoral." A month later, Harlell Jones, the leader of a group called the Afro Set, gave the City Club a primer on Black Nationalism. Black Nationalism, he said, does not mean the black man is going back to Africa. "Nationalism means *right here*," he said, going on to complain about those who say that if the black man doesn't like it here he should go back to Africa. "If you don't like what we're doing," he told the City Club audience, "go back to Europe." In February 1971, the financier Cyrus S. Eaton returned to the City Club, dismissing as "bunk" the notion that the election of a Socialist president of Chile, Salvador Allende, spelled the end of democracy. A few months later, as part of an all-day barnstorming tour to mobilize the public to pressure their elected representatives to withdraw from Vietnam, U.S. Representatives Bella Abzug, Democrat of New York, and Henry S. Reuss, Democrat of Wisconsin, joined Congressman Charles A. Vanik of Cleveland on a walk from Public Square to the City Club, where Abzug told a jam-packed forum, "Congress never declared war in Southeast Asia, but we can undeclare it . . . Congress has the power to stop the war."

it. In January 1971, the City Club membership approved a move to newly renovated quarters on the third floor of the Women's Federal Building at 320 Superior Avenue. The City Club and the Women's City Club[10] entered into an agreement to operate a shared kitchen while occupying separate dining and clubrooms. A shared kitchen would reduce each club's cost of providing daily lunch service. Following on the heels of the joint agreement, the City Club named Alan J. Davis, editorial director of WKBF-TV and a Methodist minister, to succeed Frederick A. Vierow as executive secretary. (Several months later, the board voted to change that title to executive director.) Davis, a graduate of Yale University and Yale Divinity School, told the *Plain Dealer* that he took the job because of the club's community involvement, "which is not inconsistent with my former role in the ministry."

How, in good conscience, could the City Club expect women to contribute to the support of its forums—even, on occasion, to speak at them—but deny them membership?

## A "whole new ball game"

As the 1970–71 forum season drew to a close, the City Club was on the cusp of change. Its 712 Vincent Avenue home was one of several buildings being eyed by National City Bank for possible expansion of its headquarters. The club's ground lease had expired and the property owner declined to renew

10. Founded in 1916, the Women's City Club had been in the Bulkley Building in Playhouse Square since 1934. The building was sold in 1970, and when the club's lease expired the new owner proposed a substantial increase in rent, prompting the club to relocate.

On July 9, 1971, the City Club Forum closed out forty-two years at 712 Vincent, inviting Mayor Carl B. Stokes and former Mayors Thomas A. Burke, Frank J. Lausche, Anthony J. Celebrezze, and Ralph S. Locher each to speak for ten minutes on the subject "Learning from the Past, Living in the Present." The program was billed as a forum "with a light touch." Only Locher and Stokes accepted, and the program was anything but light. Locher complained that there was too much publicity on "what is wrong with our city" and declared that what passes for "vision" in Cleveland "doesn't let us see beyond the end of our nose." Stokes, in what the *New York Times* characterized as "one of his good-by speeches to the city" (Stokes had announced earlier that year that he would not seek re-election), made amends to Locher for having been among those who "blamed him for what hadn't been done in Cleveland." He then excoriated the newspapers, which, he charged, "contribute to the city's problems by slanted coverage of the news." Stokes also assailed Cleveland's thirty-three-member city council, elected by wards, which results in "parochialism" and "a narrowness of vision." With those remarks, the City Club bade farewell to Short Vincent, a street fondly memorialized in an ode written by club member Joseph S. Newman:

> Here flourished the honky tonks, the pubs,
> The stately bank, the worthiest of clubs.

Two weeks later, a small infantry of members and officers carried the club's chairs and *objets d'art*, including the treasured Chinese gong rung to open and close each forum, down Euclid Avenue to the City Club's new home, where all were served a dollar lunch.

In offering good wishes to the City Club at its new location, the *Cleveland Plain Dealer* declared: "Conservatives and liberals—with radicals from both wings—have found the City Club a true forum of free speech." In truth, however, politically conservative club members were feeling marginalized, according to an item in Milt Widder's column of January 19, 1972, in the *Cleveland Press*. "There is a move on," he wrote, "among the conservative members of the City Club to have a more influential voice in the affairs of the men's club. They are disenchanted with the liberals who are being accused of running the weekly forums and 'stacking the deck' in favor of the liberal view." In January 1972, two conservative candidates won seats on the City Club board: Franklin A. Polk, a lawyer and onetime Republican candidate for mayor; and Robert Hughes, co-chairman of the Cuyahoga County Republican Party.

The tension between opposite ends of the political spectrum was soon eclipsed by another issue that had become, according to the *Plain Dealer*, "THE major topic of discussion at 320 Superior Avenue, N.E.": whether women should be admitted as members. The newspaper reported that, while City Club members had long debated informally the question of admitting women, the issue had been brought to a head with the applications for membership of ten women.

On February 16, 1972, the City Club held a debate on the question. Tom Campbell spoke in favor of admitting women, James B. Davis against. Campbell's speech, with its unassailable arguments, survives. It reads in part:

> Within a decade of our founding, the City Club became an institution vested with a quasi-public role. Candidates for every major office affecting the interest and well-being of Clevelanders debated on our podium and answered the questions of our members. Every major [public] issue . . . has been debated, analyzed and criticized by our members . . .
>
> And yet this great public institution, nationally and internationally renowned for its devotion to the principle of freedom and fairness of speech, contains within itself a flaw that is presently impairing its image in this community. The famous club that pioneered in opening its doors and membership to all men regardless of race, creed or color of skin, denies that opportunity to *women*—of *any* race, *any* creed or *any* skin color.
>
> . . . Our world has changed. Women are nearing the end of their long march to equality. We can no longer remain half restricted, half free. Opening our forums, but refusing to break bread. We are too sensitive, too sophisticated to stand in these portals and say to half the members of this community—thus far, and no further, shall ye come.[11]

Although the City Club then counted 1,150 members, only those present at the debate could vote. The result was 65 in favor and 63 against; passage required a two-thirds majority. Within days, City Club President Larry Robinson told the *Cleveland Plain Dealer* that the club would poll its members on the question of admitting women to membership, saying that discussion of the matter had "increased immeasurably" since the vote and that some speakers scheduled to address the forum had expressed second thoughts about appearing at a club that banned women.

Three months later, the City Club scheduled another vote on changing its bylaws to admit women—same rules, with one exception: club members would have to vote in person, but they would not have to stay during the meeting. Robinson told the *Plain Dealer* that, as a result of its men-only policy, the club was facing two threatened lawsuits, the loss of younger members, and the inability to book prominent speakers. "The choice," he said, "is whether the members want to perpetuate a men's eating club or a club with a social function of presenting public debate." A mail survey, he said, showed that 71 percent of City Club members were in favor of admitting women.

On June 2, 1972, City Club members voted 228 to 97 to admit women as members. The next day's *Cleveland Press* opined: "Yesterday, the barriers against women members were battered down . . . The club has thus re-validated its prestige and the long and honorable reputation it has enjoyed as a group of progressive thought and action . . .

Thomas F. Campbell (1924–2003), a professor of history at Cleveland State University who later co-founded the school's Institute of Urban Affairs, was an active City Club member and the author of its first history. During a debate on the admission of women to membership, he called their exclusion "a flaw that is . . . impairing [the City's Club's] image in this community." This photograph was taken in 1977, when Campbell briefly became a candidate for mayor of Cleveland. THE CLEVELAND PRESS COLLECTION, MICHAEL SCHWARTZ LIBRARY, CLEVELAND STATE UNIVERSITY

11. Campbell was a student of Irish history, and the final sentence quoted here echoes the words of the Irish national political leader Joseph Stewart Parnell (1846–1891), who, in 1885, as a member of Parliament representing Cork City, said: "No man has the right to fix the boundary of a nation. No man has the right to say to his country, 'Thus far shalt thou go and no further,' and we have never attempted to fix the 'ne plus ultra' to the progress of Ireland's nationhood, and we never shall."

On June 2, 1972, following months of debate, City Club members voted to admit women, removing a barrier that had become, wrote the *Cleveland Press*, "an embarrassing anomaly." The same day, Norma Huey, executive director of the Women's City Club (shown here with City Club President Larry Robinson), became the first woman to join. THE CLEVELAND PRESS COLLECTION, MICHAEL SCHWARTZ LIBRARY, CLEVELAND STATE UNIVERSITY

The City Club was burdened by an embarrassing anomaly as long as it kept women out." Norma Huey, executive director of the Women's City Club, became the first woman to join the City Club of Cleveland. What happened as a result of this earthshaking change in policy? "Nothing much," Larry Robinson told the *Plain Dealer* three months later. Eighteen women had joined the club and only one male member had resigned.

Among the first women to join the City Club were Nancy Cronin, Roberta Steinbacher, and Rena Blumberg. Interviewed in 2012, they shared similar recollections that the club's integration was "no big deal." "No one tried to bar me at the door," Cronin said, adding that "most [male members] were very welcoming." Cronin, a self-described "political junkie" whose career in local government included service as director of development for Cuyahoga County, was first exposed to the City Club as a teenager when her father, a lawyer and club member, would occasionally bring her to open forums. Her husband Kiely was also a member and served a term as president in 1975 (as Cronin herself would in 1983). She said she believed that the club's historic exclusion of women was less a deliberate choice than a matter of tradition—or, as she put it, "It's always been this way."

Roberta Steinbacher, a Kansas native, was new to Cleveland in 1972 when Tom Campbell, her colleague at Cleveland State University's Institute of Urban Affairs, introduced her to the City Club and even paid her dues. Steinbacher, now director of undergraduate programs at the school's Maxine Goodman Levin College of Urban Affairs, said, "In the early days, it was a way [for me] to meet new people, as well as to be informed about local, state, and national issues." Rena Blumberg's father, Ezra Z. Shapiro, was an active member of the City Club. In the early 70s, Blumberg was working as the community affairs director for radio stations WIXY-WDOK when she joined the City Club. "Women were emerging in the workplace," she recalled. "There was a sense of excitement about new opportunities [opening to women]." The association proved salutary. "It was a place to meet all kinds of people who had not been available to me before [joining]," said Blumberg (now Rena Blumberg Olshansky). "The forums were outstanding. It was *the place* to go on Fridays." In recalling their early experiences as new members of the City Club, all three women cited the club's value as a place to communicate and exchange ideas, to grow intellectually, and to meet and interact with city leaders.

The admission of women coincided with a period of vibrant activity at the City Club. Executive Director Alan Davis injected the club's management with a new, youthful spirit. He invited students from area high schools to attend and participate in the Friday forums and offered the City Club Forum as the venue for the annual high school debating championship. He hired Lillian Anderson, who had been the secretary at Berea's United Methodist Church where Davis was a minister. Anderson, an African American, was

quickly promoted to associate director. "They were a team," Dennis Dooley, a former City Club president, recalled in 2012. "They made it a warm and welcoming place. They were the face of the City Club." Also interviewed in 2012, Anderson recalled Davis, who died in 1999, as "brilliant and easygoing, with a good mind. He loved people, and he had his finger on the pulse of the city." Davis, she said, was "unruffled" if a speaker cancelled at the last minute. "And he was creative," she added, citing club-sponsored trips to London, Paris, the Soviet Union, and other locales, where Davis arranged forums featuring local speakers.

In 1972, the club was enjoying its spacious and modern new home in the Women's Federal Building. The podium— so it seemed in that presidential election year—was continuously occupied by a figure of prominence, including, on October 25, Senator George McGovern, Democrat of South Dakota, the first presidential candidate of a major party to address the City Club Forum. In fact, wrote Bud Weidenthal in the *Cleveland Press*, the City Club was "so deluged with activity that only passing note will be taken of [its] 60th anniversary milestone on October 28"; the club's lineup of speakers, he wrote, would stand in lieu of any special observance. A partial list included R. Sargent Shriver (Senator McGovern's running mate); former U.S. Attorney General Ramsey Clark; George P. Shultz, secretary of the treasury; John H. Connelly, former treasury secretary; Senator Edmund S. Muskie, Democrat of Maine; Leonard Woodcock, president of the United Auto Workers; L. Patrick Gray III, acting director of the FBI; George H.

**The podium—so it seemed in that presidential election year—was continuously occupied by a figure of prominence.**

On October 5, 1972, Senator George McGovern, the Democratic candidate for president, addressed the City Club, the first among many prominent speakers who appeared during a pivotal year. Occupying new quarters, under new leadership, and with its membership rolls now open to women, the club gained a new vibrancy. City Club President Larry Robinson, seen at lower left, played a significant role in moving the club forward. THE CITY CLUB OF CLEVELAND

W. Bush, U.S. ambassador to the United Nations; and Jean M. Westwood, Democratic national chairwoman. So much activity, Weidenthal wrote, contrasted with the observance of the club's 50th anniversary a decade earlier in the "drab surroundings of its aging Short Vincent headquarters," when an editorial writer from Washington gave "an appropriate speech on freedom of the press before an all-male audience. It seemed as if the club was living in the past . . . The older men still played cards in the back room, the paneled library upstairs was used mostly by tired lawyers and businessmen for noontime catnaps on the soft leather couches." A decade later, Weidenthal added, "it's like a whole new ball game."

A whole new ball game indeed. In December 1972, Bert Gardner, vice president of urban affairs at the Cleveland Trust Company, was elected president of the City Club, the first African American to hold that office. The following October, two women—Rena Blumberg and Vilma Kohn, an attorney with Squire, Sanders and Dempsey—were among eight nominees for four seats on the board of trustees. Both won, and in 1975 Blumberg would be elected vice president of the City Club, becoming its first female officer. Three years later, attorney Annette Butler, an African American, would become the club's first female president. By 1975, about 150 women had joined the City Club, constituting just over 10 percent of the total membership. In 1976, the board of trustees voted to eliminate the requirement of a sponsor for membership; the club would now be open to anyone having an interest in its activities.

The issues that preoccupied America in the 1970s—ending the Vietnam War, race relations, nuclear proliferation, the energy crisis, abortion rights, and equal rights for women—all were aired at the City Club Forum. A succession of provocative voices appeared at the club's podium during this culturally and politically convulsive period. Among them were the Reverend Philip Berrigan, recently released from prison for burning draft records in protest of the war; Russell Means, leader of the American Indian Movement, then traveling the country to raise money for the Wounded Knee Defense Fund; farm labor organizer Cesar Chavez, speaking on the national lettuce boycott; and actress Jane Fonda, who delivered a passionate indictment of the war in Vietnam, denounced South Vietnam as a "police state" created by U.S. dollars "in the name of peace with honor," and called Secretary of State Henry Kissinger (who had just won the Nobel Peace Prize) "a killer with blood on his hands."

The City Club hosted a young Democratic senator from Delaware named Joseph R. Biden Jr. and, one year before he disappeared, Jimmy Hoffa, the former president of the International Brotherhood of Teamsters. Barbara Mikulski, then a member of the Baltimore City Council—she would later chair the powerful House Appropriations Committee—spoke on "The Blue-Collar Woman." Also on the roster were Hortensia Bussi de Allende, the widow of Salvador Allende, the deposed president of Chile (visibly irritated by her questioners, she abruptly terminated the forum), John Kenneth Galbraith, Fred Friendly, Norman Podhoretz, Frank Robinson, David Broder, Vernon Jordan, Karen DeCrow, General Elmo R. Zumwalt, and Nguyễn

On Candidates' Night, November 19, 1973, Vilma Kohn, left, and Rena Blumberg make their pitch for votes, with good-natured opposition from fellow candidate Joseph Fowler. Kohn and Blumberg were both elected, becoming the first women to serve as trustees. THE CLEVELAND PRESS COLLECTION, MICHAEL SCHWARTZ LIBRARY, CLEVELAND STATE UNIVERSITY

City Club President Annette Butler presides at the debate among a large field of Democratic primary candidates for Congress, May 9, 1980. Butler was the first woman to serve as president of the City Club. THE CLEVELAND PRESS COLLECTION, MICHAEL SCHWARTZ LIBRARY, CLEVELAND STATE UNIVERSITY

Nguyễn Cao Kỳ, the former prime minister of South Vietnam, meets with high school students following his speech at the City Club Forum, December 5, 1975. THE CLEVELAND PRESS COLLECTION, MICHAEL SCHWARTZ LIBRARY, CLEVELAND STATE UNIVERSITY

**A brash young reformer, Cleveland Councilman Dennis Kucinich, used the City Club podium to champion preservation of the city's Municipal Electric Light Plant, a legacy of Mayor Tom L. Johnson.**

12. In 1970, WCLV-FM had taken over live radio broadcast of the City Club Forum from WGAR, which was changing its format; other local stations repeated the broadcast each weekend.

Cao Kỳ, the former prime minister of South Vietnam. The club did not shy from speakers whose messages might rankle or anger, hosting the physicist and inventor William Shockley, a proponent of eugenics; Phyllis Schlafly, an outspoken opponent of feminism and the proposed Equal Rights Amendment; and Lester Maddox, the former governor of Georgia and a onetime segregationist.

Local issues continued to receive a thorough airing. A brash young reformer, Cleveland Councilman Dennis Kucinich, used the City Club podium to champion preservation of the city's Municipal Electric Light Plant, a legacy of Mayor Tom L. Johnson. Kucinich's subsequent election as mayor was soon followed by an effort to recall him, leading to a City Club debate on the recall movement between Tom Campbell (for the recall) and Ted Bonda (against). (Kucinich was not recalled.) Court-ordered busing of the city's schoolchildren to achieve desegregation was explained, damned, rationalized, and justified by a succession of forum speakers and panelists. In 1976, in the Q & A following a talk by the leaders of several Cleveland banks, City Club President Bob Cavano, a proponent of racial integration and a proud regular at the Soviet Table, pressed them to stop redlining and to disclose the addresses of loan recipients.

In the spring of 1976, another presidential candidate, Governor Jimmy Carter of Georgia, addressed the City Club. His Democratic primary opponents, Senators Frank Church and Morris Udall, also made appearances. James J. Bambrick, a labor relations expert and devoted City Club member, used his professional friendships to bring AFL-CIO President John Sweeney and, over the years, three presidents of the United Steelworkers to speak at the club. The decade closed with a remarkable lineup of speakers, including FBI Director William Webster, newspaper columnist Jack Anderson, the conservative author and commentator William F. Buckley Jr., business magnate Armand Hammer (the chairman of Occidental Petroleum spoke on "Oil Shale—Practical Answer to Fuel Problem"), Yankees owner George Steinbrenner, and Maynard Jackson, the first African American mayor of Atlanta, Georgia.

Beginning in 1979, the City Club extended its reach as a professional crew from the television department of Cuyahoga Community College began videotaping forum programs for broadcast on Saturday over WVIZ-TV, Cleveland's public television station. In March the following year, City Club Forum radio broadcasts went national when a talk by Bishop Thomas J. Gumbleton of Detroit, one of three American clergymen who had visited the U.S. hostages in Tehran at Christmas, was transmitted via satellite to twenty-one National Public Radio (NPR) stations.[12] (In the question-and-answer period, Gumbleton said the United States should admit its error in backing the deposed Shah Mohammad Reza Pahlevi.) By 1987, broadcasts of the City Club Forum were being distributed to more than one hundred NPR stations in thirty-eight states and the District of Columbia, reaching as far as KCAW in Sitka, Alaska.

THE CITY CLUB OF CLEVELAND □ THE WOMEN'S CITY CLUB OF CLEVELAND

In 1982, downtown redevelopment once again caused the City Club to search for a new home. The Women's Federal Building, which it had occupied since 1971, was to be demolished to make way for the new Standard Oil Company (Ohio) headquarters. In March, board members of both the City Club and the Women's City Club voted to relocate to shared quarters on the second floor of the Citizens Building, a Beaux Arts office tower at 850 Euclid Avenue that housed the city's gem and jewelry trade. Proceeds from the lease buyout paid for the outfitting of new clubrooms. In January 1983, more than a thousand members and guests attended an opening reception at the new facility, where they admired designer Ray W. Clarke's palette of "rosy taupe, malachite green, and salmon" and the eclectic mix of neo-Regency furniture with vintage upholstered pieces covered in "pigskin vinyl" from the club's Short Vincent days. "It's warm and inviting and has scads of ambience," *Plain Dealer* society columnist Mary Strassmeyer gushed.

The quality and variety of City Club programming continued seamlessly, with appearances by Dick Gregory, Seymour Hersh, Betty Friedan, William Safire, James Meredith, the Reverend Jerry Falwell, Senator Ted Kennedy, William Sloane Coffin, the Reverend Joseph E. Lowery, and Vice President George Bush. As chairman of the program

In January 1983, the City Club of Cleveland moved to the Citizens Building at 850 Euclid Avenue. Sharing a celebratory moment at the open house were, left to right, Robert Gaede, architect of the renovation, City Club President Nelson Weiss, Executive Director Alan J. Davis, and Ray Clarke, interior designer. THE CITY CLUB OF CLEVELAND

> **Owing to his frailty, Ashley Montagu, an eminent social biologist and humanist, sat behind a desk as he spoke, his quiet brilliance causing one longtime member to recall, a quarter of a century later, that "his intellect intimidated the entire audience."**

committee in the late 1980s, Dennis Dooley, an editor and writer then working at the Cleveland Foundation, brought Rosa Parks to the City Club podium, as well as a number of past recipients of the Anisfield-Wolf Book Award, including Lucy Dawidowicz, Claude Brown, and Ashley Montagu. In a 2012 interview, Dooley remembered feeling moved by the acclamation Rosa Parks received from the City Club audience as it acknowledged a woman whose simple act of defiance—her refusal, in 1955, to give up her seat on a Montgomery, Alabama, bus to a white passenger—had made her an international symbol of resistance to racial segregation. Owing to his frailty, Montagu, an eminent social biologist and humanist, sat behind a desk as he spoke, his quiet brilliance causing longtime member Bob Lustig to recall, a quarter of a century later, that "his intellect intimidated the entire audience." In the Q & A, asked to sum up a lifetime of wisdom and learning, Montagu answered quietly, "Love one another."

Star power did not come cheap. Guidelines established by the board in 1979 authorized the club to pay speakers their travel expenses and an honorarium of $500. Although, in practice, honoraria were rarely given, other costs were rising and the club began to struggle financially. In anticipation of the City Club's 75th anniversary in 1987, Stanley Adelstein, president of the City Club Forum Foundation, conceived the idea of the funded forum: in exchange for a donation of $25,000, an individual donor would enjoy the distinction of having an annual forum named in his or her honor. "Stanley showed extraordinary leadership in developing the concept of the dedicated forum, and he single-handedly recruited a large number of donors," longtime member Rick Taft would later recall. "This moved the Forum Foundation endowment from modest to consequential and assured that the City Club could weather a financial storm." By the time of the City Club's 75th anniversary celebration in October 1987, Adelstein and his blue-ribbon committee had persuaded twenty-seven people to endow forums, bringing $675,000 into foundation coffers and protecting the future of the club's renowned forum.[13]

To recognize the extraordinary contributions of its most devoted members, in 1985 the City Club Hall of Fame was established. The first four inductees were honored at a May banquet featuring *Washington Post* columnist David Broder as guest speaker. Those honored were Daniel E. Morgan (1877–1949), city manager, judge, civic reformer, and the first president of the City Club; Peter Witt (1869–1948), street railroad commissioner under Mayor Newton D. Baker and later a city councilman; Carl D. Friebolin (1878–1967), noted for creating, writing, and producing the club's annual Anvil Revue; and Philip W. Porter (1900–1985), retired executive editor of the *Plain Dealer* and a founder of the City Club Forum Foundation. Two years later, a second round of inductions, this time with National Public Radio commentator Daniel Schorr doing the honors as banquet speaker, added Newton D. Baker (1871–1937),

13. By 2013, the number of endowed forums had grown to forty-five. Early donors were able to specify the subject of the forum. Adelstein and his wife Hope, for example, endowed "The Stanley and Hope Adelstein Endowed Forum on the Environment." Other donors funded forums on such subjects as health care, civil liberties, national politics, and the American economy. The cost of an endowed forum has since risen to $50,000 and the subject can no longer be specified.

Jack Raper (1870–1950), Joseph Newman (1891–1960), and Peter DiLeone. Only DiLeone was alive to enjoy the applause. A respected labor lawyer and unabashed liberal active in Democratic politics, DiLeone was a pillar of the City Club who presided at the Soviet Table, where his passion for discussion and debate made lunch, one intimate later recalled, a "meal for both the stomach and the mind."

To mark the 75th anniversary of the nation's longest-running free speech forum, Rena Blumberg, together with co-chair Paul Unger and club program chair Dennis Dooley, conceived a monumental event, two years in the making, with the theme "The Power of Ideas." Twenty-five years later, in a 2012 interview, Blumberg recalled the event as if it were yesterday. "We selected eight outstanding speakers," she explained, "each of whom was sponsored for a daylong visit by a different Cleveland company or organization. Each was also charged with presenting [at the club's evening gala], in five minutes' time, *one idea.*" On the night of October 28, 1987, Blumberg greeted the 1,474 guests gathered in the ballroom of the Stouffer Tower City Plaza Hotel, saying, "This is the greatest gathering of minds since Thomas Jefferson dined alone at the White House" before introducing the guest speakers as they descended a spiral staircase: Gloria Steinem, New York Governor Mario Cuomo, T. Boone Pickens, Eleanor Holmes Norton, John Kenneth Galbraith, Phil Donahue, and Jeane Kirkpatrick.[14] The event was front-page news and a triumph for the City Club.

On February 10, 1988, the City Club Forum hosted its first sitting president when President Ronald Reagan asked for an opportunity to present an address on his economic policy to the club. THE CITY CLUB OF CLEVELAND

14. Wall Street financier Felix Rohatyn, one of the eight guest speakers, was unable to attend due to illness.

On February 10, 1988, the City Club Forum hosted its first sitting president when President Ronald Reagan asked for an opportunity to present an address on his economic policy to the club. In December, an advance team of thirty visited Cleveland to work out the details with Executive Director Alan Davis and (owing to club President David Sindell's illness) Vice President Bruce Akers. One week before the president's talk, another group arrived to hold daily briefings with Davis and Akers, and to put into place elaborate security measures at the Stouffer Tower City Hotel, the site of the speech.

Akers later recalled some of the precautions taken to protect the president, who, in 1981, had survived an assassination attempt. On the dais, the tablecloth concealed a steel plate in front of Mr. Reagan; the "waiters" who served the head table were, in fact, Secret Service agents; and the president's plate of food was assembled at random from others' plates. The president was seated between Akers and Cleveland Mayor George V. Voinovich. Akers recalled asking the president who, among the world's leaders, had made the greatest impression on him. He named two: Margaret Thatcher and Anwar Sadat. Mr. Reagan singled out Mrs. Thatcher's great wit, recalling that at the G8 Summit in Williamsburg, Virginia, in 1985, he started to say, "If your King George had not been so stubborn . . ." Thatcher finished his sentence, saying, ". . . then I'd be hosting *you* tonight!"

President Ronald Reagan was the first sitting president to address the City Club of Cleveland. The event, held at the Stouffer Tower City Hotel on Public Square, was a sellout. Following the speech, City Club Vice President Bruce Akers (standing to the right of the president) presented the president with a football signed by Browns quarterback Bernie Kosar and a customized sweatshirt. "The place went wild," Akers later recalled. THE CITY CLUB OF CLEVELAND

CLEVELAND CITY CLUB

Owing to the club's stature and media reach, an aspirant to public office seldom refused an invitation to debate at the City Club. In September 1989, it was the setting for a dramatic, even pivotal contest among the five candidates in Cleveland's nonpartisan mayoral primary. The room was filled to overflowing as Council President George L. Forbes, the presumed frontrunner, boasted in his opening statement of the municipal progress he and Mayor George V. Voinovich had made in the previous decade and promised "continuity." His oratorically gifted opponent, State Senator Michael R. White, seized on the word like a cudgel. "Continuity won't do," White asserted repeatedly, employing the staccato style favored by some African American preachers and earning thunderous applause as he called for better public safety, housing, education, and race relations. White's performance that day lifted him above the crowded field, putting him into a two-man contest with Forbes that he would win handily in November. "The Mike White-Forbes [primary] debate at the City Club absolutely changed the election results," one eyewitness, City Club regular Bob Lustig, later recalled. White went on to become the longest-serving mayor in Cleveland history, earning plaudits for such large new developments as the Rock and Roll Hall of Fame and the Gateway project—which brought the city a new professional baseball stadium and basketball arena—even as he presided, throughout the 1990s, over a stubbornly troubled city.

Mayoral candidate Michael R. White tells a City Club audience "continuity won't do" in solving the city's problems. Looking on, from left, are rivals Ralph J. Perk Jr., George L. Forbes, and Benny Bonanno. CHRIS STEPHENS/PLAIN DEALER/LANDOV

## Righting the ship

In anticipation of Executive Director Alan Davis's retirement, City Club trustees sought to ensure a smooth transition. In 1993, Bruce Akers, then mayor of the Cleveland suburb of Pepper Pike, headed a search committee to find a managing director who could learn the ropes before taking over from Davis. The club hired James H. "Jim" Foster, an affable executive who grew up in Shaker Heights, graduated from Kenyon College, and spent thirteen years in the Air National Guard flying F-100s and F-84s out of a unit in Mansfield while working full time in advertising. He later joined a two-man company that produced air shows around the country. Foster's strong background as an event planner and organizer suited him for the job.

Foster stepped into the top post on July 1, 1994. Looking back in 2013, he described a club that was listing under leadership "that operated on the business model that 'God would provide.'" The club's finances were shaky, its administrative systems were archaic, and the food was terrible. Foster dug in, devoting his energies to "doing a lot of things we needed to do to make the City Club operate in a more businesslike fashion."

With generous assistance from the George Gund Foundation, Foster hired the club's first development director. (In recent years, the annual fund campaign had been a volunteer operation managed by club member Jim Bambrick.) Foster secured the club's designation as a 501(c)(3) organization and instituted corporate and nonprofit memberships in the belief that there was, as he put it, "room

> **60 Minutes reporter Mike Wallace stood and asked Silverman about the undisclosed payments pledged to Blue Cross's former trustees.**

at the City Club podium for the voice that corporations represent." (Alan Davis had resisted taking money from the business community, fearing that by doing so the City Club would compromise its independence.) Over time, he computerized management operations, established a presence on the World Wide Web, and, after overhearing a club member apologize to a speaker by saying, "We're known for our speakers, not for our food," terminated the club's food-service contract and selected another provider. In Foster's words, "Food should complement the experience" of attending City Club programs.

Shortly after becoming executive director, Foster got the surprise of his life—a call from the White House. President Bill Clinton wanted to give a speech at the City Club. Clinton had spoken at the City Club twice before—in 1992, as governor of Arkansas and a presidential candidate, and again in 1993, as president—and had a high regard for the venue. In advance of the program, Representative Martin Hoke, a freshman Republican who represented a congressional district on Cleveland's West Side, beseeched Jim Foster, an old schoolmate, for an opportunity to pose a question to the president in the Q & A following his talk. Foster explained that Hoke, like everyone else hoping to ask a question, would have to put his name into a fishbowl and go with the luck of the draw.

On October 24, 1994, only days before the mid-term elections that would see a historic shift of power in Congress in the Republicans' favor, Clinton addressed an audience of 780 at the Statler Office Tower. It was, the *Cleveland Plain Dealer*'s Mary Anne Sharkey later reported, "a solid speech about the accomplishments of his administration," and the mostly Democratic crowd gave him a warm welcome. When the president concluded his speech, the City Club's Lillian Anderson picked the name of the first questioner: Martin Hoke! Hoke proceeded to grandstand, accusing Clinton of using "inflammatory" language by calling the "Contract with America" (the G.O.P.'s legislative initiative) a "contract *on* America." "At a time when the public is so concerned about violent crime," Hoke said, "why would you resort to using such talk?" Clinton, "like a sheriff with a lynch mob," Sharkey wrote, held back the openly hostile crowd, many of whom were imploring the president to ignore Hoke's remark. Addressing Hoke, Clinton said, "I appreciate your concern about crime and violence. I wish you hadn't voted against the Brady bill and the crime bill." The crowd roared its appreciation of the president's verbal coup. "Clinton buried Hoke," City Club member Bob Lustig recalled almost twenty years later.

Lustig, a regular at the City Club since joining in 1964, recalled another incident of high drama. He was presiding over a debate at the City Club Forum on August 30, 1996. The subject was the proposed sale of the nonprofit Blue Cross & Blue Shield of Ohio to the for-profit Columbia/HCA Healthcare Corporation. A lawyer representing Families USA, a nonprofit advocate of affordable health care, led off, criticizing the deal—a deal that Ohio Attorney General Betty Montgomery was then battling in court—for its low sales price, lucrative payouts to the insurer's top officers, and retirement benefits to be paid to its former trustees. Blue Cross Chairman John Burry Jr. had backed out of his commitment to appear at the City Club, and speaking on behalf of Blue Cross was PR man William Silverman. Silverman completely sidestepped the subject, talking instead about his mother's recent fall and the changes under way in the health care industry.

Unbeknown to Lustig and most others, a crew from CBS News was seated at one of the tables. During the question-and-answer period, *60 Minutes* reporter Mike Wallace stood and asked Silverman about the undisclosed payments pledged to Blue Cross's former trustees. Silverman "ducked, bobbed, and weaved," Lustig said, angering the audience, some of whom shouted, "Answer the question!" At the end of the forum, the crowd was on its feet, cheering as Silverman fled the room with the television crew in hot pursuit. "There is no doubt in my mind," Lustig said in 2013, "that public reaction to the City Club Forum helped to kill the deal [between Blue Cross and Columbia/HCA]."

Although the tradition of Candidates' Night had come to an end in the 1970s, election to the board of trustees continued to be contested, a custom some found anachronistic if not humiliating. Shortly after becoming executive director, Jim Foster telephoned Richard W. "Dick" Pogue to ask him to consider joining the board of trustees. Although Pogue had been a member of the City Club since 1964, he had never been active. Foster explained, sheepishly, that Pogue—then the managing partner of Jones Day, one of the largest law firms in the world, and a Cleveland power broker—would be expected to run for the seat as part of a field of eight candidates; the top four vote-getters would win election. Pogue took a dim view of the process but agreed to go along with it—and won. As a trustee, he later persuaded the board to modernize the club's board selection procedures and bring them into line with those of other civic organizations. Going forward, the board would nominate only enough candidates to fill the open seats, though additional nominations from the membership would require only a handful of signatures. Pogue's reform was well-received and, since its implementation, contested elections have been rare.

Pogue's addition to the board had another discernible effect. "The City Club's reputation had become so liberal," Pogue said in a 2012 interview, "that it was hard to get conservative speakers to appear at its podium. I believed freedom of speech meant having a balanced program." Other members of long standing viewed the situation differently. Bruce Akers, a staunch Republican, put it bluntly, "Conservative speakers want to be paid." That observation was echoed by Rick Taft, a Democrat, who, when he served as program chair, found it much easier to get liberal speakers. "Liberals want to stir up the populace," he said, and are happy to speak without compensation, while conserva-

> "The City Club's reputation had become so liberal that it was hard to get conservative speakers to appear at its podium. I believed freedom of speech meant having a balanced program."
> —Richard W. Pogue

Following the successful negotiation of a new lease in 1999, the owner of the Citizens Building, where the City Club had made its home since 1983, agreed to change its name to the City Club Building. THE CITY CLUB OF CLEVELAND

Marking the start of demolition in preparation for the City Club's makeover, November 1999, are, left to right, Executive Director Jim Foster; Dick Pogue, project visionary and co-chair of the capital campaign; City Club President Brian D. Tucker; and architect Robert Bostwick. THE CITY CLUB OF CLEVELAND

Dick Pogue, at the podium, ushered in a new era as he welcomed members and guests to the first forum following the City Club's renovation, May 12, 2000. Together with Hank Doll, Pogue co-chaired the capital campaign that financed the $2 million project. *Washington Post* columnist David Broder, seated, was the featured speaker that day. THE CITY CLUB OF CLEVELAND

tives "have a 'market' view of life and expect to be paid." Determined to press for balance, Pogue succeeded in attracting high-profile business and conservative leaders, such as Steven Brill, the founder and publisher of *American Lawyer* magazine, House Republican Leader John Boehner, former Senator Alan Simpson, and President George W. Bush. (In 1993, even before joining the board, Pogue, through his professional association with Arkansas businessman Thomas F. "Mack" McLarty III, the White House chief of staff for President Bill Clinton, had arranged for President Clinton to address the City Club in May 1993, his first of two appearances as President.) Pogue would prove instrumental, too, in a wholly different realm.

## Toward a larger purpose

In 1998, the City Club's lease on its space in the Citizens Building was running out. The Women's City Club, hemorrhaging members and no longer able to afford its share of the rent, in 1990 had departed the space it had agreed to share with the City Club. The club's facilities had become dated and shabby. In a 2012 interview, Jim Foster recalled telling then City Club President Dick Pogue, "It looks like an old white men's club." Pogue agreed that the City Club deserved to have a home that measured up to the caliber of its speakers. A determined search for other quarters yielded nothing to rival the Citizens Building with its central location and adjacent parking. "OK," Pogue told Foster, "but if we stay

we ought to raise two million dollars and do it right." Pogue obtained a commitment of $250,000 from the Cleveland Foundation—bolstering the club's confidence in proceeding with the project—and, together with Hank Doll, co-chaired the fundraising campaign, eventually exceeding his $2 million goal. Working pro bono, Rick Taft negotiated a new lease with the building owner that was attractive enough to justify the investment. To sweeten the deal and retain a valued tenant, the building owner agreed to change its name to the City Club Building.

Meanwhile, the City Club Forum Foundation provided $50,000 to hire an architect to prepare a preliminary design and renderings. Members of the renovation committee, chaired by Ron Tober, sat down with architect Robert Bostwick. In a 2012 interview, Art Brooks, a veteran City Club member who served on the committee, recalled committee member Bill Bolton's astute suggestion that, in approaching the project, the question to be addressed was "How would you express the notion of free speech in architecture?" Bostwick responded by creating bright, open, and contemporary spaces attuned to the club's functional needs, including a lobby generous enough to foster post-forum debate and conversation. An expanse of glass doors, etched with the names of hundreds of those who have addressed the City Club since 1912, visually connected the lobby through a dining room to the windows overlooking Euclid Avenue and, symbolically, the city outside. In the auditorium, the podium was repositioned from the narrow end of the rectangular room to its broad side, allowing greater proximity and

intimacy between speaker and audience. The beloved Elmer Brown mural was returned to the auditorium and restored.[15]

The renovation was "transformative," Jim Foster said in 2012. Gone was any trace of the private men's eating club of yore. The redesigned space better met the club's operational needs, gave it a fresh new face, and subtly shifted the club's focus from eating club to speakers' platform. Foster credited Dick Pogue for his vision; Cleveland architect Thomas T. K. Zung for helping to guide the project; and Ron Tober for leading the renovation committee. Following the Friday forum of October 31, 1999, the City Club moved to temporary quarters in the Huntington Building across the street to permit the old space to be gutted and the new quarters built. Six months later, on May 12, 2000, three hundred people attended the dedication of the new facility at a sold-out forum featuring David Broder, the longtime *Washington Post* politics writer and a friend of the City Club.

In 2001, the City Club devoted a series of forums to civic and social issues challenging Greater Cleveland. The first, on regional development, was scheduled for Wednesday, September 12. Then came the terrorist attacks of 9/11, shocking the nation and the world. City Club President Leonard M. Calabrese conferred with Jim Foster. "We were of the same mind," Calabrese would later recall, "—that the club's core mission of civic, civil dialogue was an excellent response to the horror," and the forum should proceed as planned. That decision, he said, "was not without pushback from a few members and from one panelist who did not participate. But proceed we did, along with a moment of

The faces of leadership: Those who have served as president of the City Club and/or the City Club Forum Foundation gathered for a photograph on September 28, 2001. Top row (left to right): Frederick I. Taft, Stanley I. Adelstein, Paul A. Unger, Brian D. Tucker, Njeri Nuru-Holm, William J. Woestendiek, Annette Butler, Thomas F. Campbell, Dennis J. Dooley, Chester J. Gray, Sheldon L. Braverman, Morton G. Epstein, Arthur V. N. Brooks, Bertram E. Gardner. Foreground (left to right): Henry C. Doll, Scott C. Finerman, Anthony C. Peebles, Nancy C. Cronin, Robert R. Cavano, Leonard M. Calabrese. THE CITY CLUB OF CLEVELAND

15. Alas, the famous Soviet Table was retired. Shorn of its legs and reduced in circumference, it is now displayed on a dining room wall as an artifact of a bygone era of long lunches and spirited chatter.

Addressing a large City Club audience at the Marriott at Key Center on March 19, 2003, Supreme Court Justice Antonin Scalia generated controversy by prohibiting the recording of his speech in its entirety. Scalia was there to receive the club's Citadel of Free Speech Award. THE CITY CLUB OF CLEVELAND

silence for all those killed and for all those continuing to respond, and a short statement in my opening [introduction] about why we were proceeding." When Health and Human Services Secretary Tommy Thompson, scheduled to speak on Friday, September 14, canceled, Foster and Calabrese hastily assembled a replacement program: a panel, consisting of a first responder, a representative of the Red Cross, a religious leader, and a child psychologist, addressed the topic "Responding to Tragedy." Calabrese later received several letters commending the City Club for its handling of a difficult week.

In March 2003, the City Club found itself at the center of a tempest. The club was to host Antonin Scalia, associate justice of the Supreme Court, at a weekday luncheon in the Grand Ballroom of the Marriott at Key Center, where he was to receive the City Club's Citadel of Free Speech Award in recognition of his spirited opinions in defense of the First Amendment. It was a homecoming of sorts: Scalia had begun his law career in Cleveland in 1961 as an associate at the Jones Day law firm, and his old colleague Dick Pogue had persuaded him to accept the award and address the City Club.

In advance of Scalia's visit, his office telephoned Jim Foster to advise him that the justice does not allow his speeches to be recorded in their entirety. Aware that WVIZ, which regularly recorded the club's Friday forums for later broadcast, had already indicated that it did not plan to record Scalia's weekday speech, Foster saw no problem agreeing to the request. Then the cable television network C-SPAN got wind of Scalia's demand and protested to both the City Club and the *Cleveland Plain Dealer*. In an editorial, the newspaper took Scalia and the City Club to task: "Scalia enjoys lifetime tenure and need never speak in public. But when he does, he, like anyone else exercising free speech, must realize that a free press has a right to report what he says." It chastised the City Club for accommodating the jurist's demands, adding, "The fact that the City Club was giving Scalia its Citadel of Free Speech Award made its capitulation all the more ironic."

In reporting the speech, the *Cleveland Plain Dealer* wrote: "Video and still cameras were swept out of the room—at Scalia's insistence—after they photographed him receiving the free-speech award." Foster saw it differently, insisting, in a 2013 interview, that "television cameras were in the room during the speech," as were photographers and radio broadcasters, "just not for the *entirety* of the speech." The incident, which elicited "lots of negative blowback from [City Club] members," according to Foster, proved to be a teachable moment. Foster resolved, with the strong consensus of the board, henceforth to be "bedrock-firm" on the fact that City Club forums "are open without any restrictions."

The Scalia imbroglio aside, Jim Foster earned accolades for his ability to present diverse programs, often of compelling interest. He has likened program planning to working a Rubik's Cube: in lieu of colors, he must match up desirable qualities. "Forum programs should be relevant, newsworthy, interesting, and high-profile when possible," he said in a 2012 interview. Foster, to good reviews, moved beyond the time-honored Friday forums, introducing flexible scheduling, such as the Friday breakfast forum that accommodated Senator Tom Daschle and the Monday dinner forum featuring Prince Bandar bin Sultan, Saudi Arabia's ambassador to the United States (both in 2003). This enabled the club to host more speakers, especially high-profile speakers who would otherwise have been unable to appear. Among those who have appeared outside the Friday noontime slot have been Jesse Jackson, Kathleen Kennedy Townsend, Enrique Peñalosa (an urban theorist and former mayor of Bogotá, Columbia), Richard Holbrooke, Madeleine Albright, Tracy Kidder, George Soros, the urban theorist Richard Florida, and Nancy Pelosi, the Democratic leader of the House of Representatives. On Monday, March 26, 2007, four days after announcing, with her husband, former Senator John Edwards, that her breast cancer had returned, but that his campaign for the presidency would continue as before, Elizabeth Edwards addressed a breakfast forum at the City Club. Foster has also introduced sponsored forums—such as the KeyBank Diversity Thought Leadership Series and the Huntington Bank Business Leaders Series—in cooperation with its corporate partners.

**Foster resolved, with the strong consensus of the board, henceforth to be "bedrock-firm" on the fact that City Club forums "are open without any restrictions."**

Executive Director Jim Foster welcomed Nancy Pelosi, the Democratic leader of the House of Representatives, prior to her appearance at a sold-out breakfast forum on April 15, 2013. Joining him were, left to right, Sandra Pianalto, chief executive of the Fourth District Federal Reserve Bank; Hewitt Shaw, managing partner of the Cleveland office of BakerHostetler; and Beth E. Mooney, chairman, chief executive officer, and president of KeyCorp. THE CITY CLUB OF CLEVELAND

The City Club of Cleveland celebrated its centennial at a gala held at the Renaissance Cleveland Hotel, October 18, 2012. Following dinner, Paula A. Kerger, president and chief executive officer of PBS, moderated a panel discussion on "The Power of Ideas to Transform Communities." Panelists included Beth E. Mooney (on monitor), chairman, chief executive officer, and president of KeyCorp; Delos "Toby" Cosgrove, M.D., chief executive officer and president of the Cleveland Clinic; Dan Gilbert, founder and chairman of Rock Ventures, Rock Gaming, and Quicken Loans and majority owner of the NBA's Cleveland Cavaliers; Alberto Ibargüen, president and chief executive officer of the John S. and James L. Knight Foundation; and Cleveland Mayor Frank G. Jackson. THE CITY CLUB OF CLEVELAND

Foster's predecessor, Alan Davis, had begun the practice of inviting high school students to attend Friday forums during the school year. By 2012, more than ten thousand high school students had participated in its programs, following which they often enjoyed their own meeting with the featured speaker. Impressed by how bright and knowledgeable many of these young people were, Foster put his own stamp on their involvement with the City Club by establishing a Youth Forum Council comprising students who plan and execute their own forum programs. Under the direction of the City Club's Catalina Quiñonez, four times each year the students select and invite speakers, make logistical and travel arrangements, and even introduce the featured speaker. Student forums have featured a U.S. senator and a Nobel laureate, among others.

City Club presentations have always covered a broad spectrum. Memorable programs in the recent past, as recalled by longtime members, included an appearance by junk-bond trader (and convicted felon) Michael Milken, who ran out the clock, precluding questions; and a profanity-laced talk by F. X. Toole (the pen name of boxing trainer Jerry Boyd), who was in Cleveland to accept the Anisfield-Wolf Book Award for *Rope Burns: Stories from the Corner*. In 2002, Cardinal Theodore McCarrick, archbishop of Washington, came to Cleveland directly from the Vatican following a meeting of the cardinalate with Pope John Paul II convened to address the growing sex-abuse crisis in the American Catholic Church. McCarrick momentarily set aside his prepared remarks (on international human rights) to brief his City Club audience on the meeting.

In the spring of 2002, Hassan Abdel Rahman, the chief representative of the Palestine Liberation Organization in the United States, addressed seven hundred City Club members and guests, amid tight security, at the Sheraton City Centre Hotel. "The response to even scheduling him was very heated and emotional," Len Calabrese, then club president, later recalled. "It turned out to be quite a civil dialogue, but I also remember receiving letters denouncing us for hosting a 'terrorist.' A few of the letters came from longtime members and donors."

Some of the most striking City Club programs have featured speakers who were little known, such as the 1994 appearance by Ronald S. McNeil, head of the American Indian College Fund and the grandson of Geronimo, who movingly described his agency's role in funding higher education for Native Americans. McNeil's talk, to an audience of just 128, contrasted with another forum, three days later, featuring House Speaker Newt Gingrich, then at the height of his political power, who addressed an audience of one thousand at the Stouffer Tower City Plaza Hotel. The juxtaposition of the two forums, Jim Foster would later say, "represented the City Club at its finest."

During Foster's tenure, Cleveland endured a decline in downtown employment which, together with the financial crisis of 2008 and the ensuing recession, caused City Club membership to erode. In a 2012 interview, Foster cited other factors as well, including outmigration and a general decline in civic participation—"the American art of association" that Alexis de Tocqueville had praised as a defining national characteristic. "The City Club exists to bring people together," Foster told the *Cleveland Plain Dealer* in 2000, "and it has become increasingly difficult to bring people downtown or out of their offices." Add to this, Foster said, the perennial challenge of booking speakers willing to appear for free. "There is so much over which we have no control. But," he added with a note of hope, "pendulums swing."

In 2012, the City Club of Cleveland marked its centennial with a year-long schedule of activities. An encore speaker series brought back compelling speakers from prior years, including Dr. Francis Collins, now the director of the National Institutes of Health, who led the Human Genome Project. An all-day conference on free speech brought together high-profile speakers from the media, politics, law, and the arts to discuss free speech in multiple contexts: the rise of the Internet, the age of terrorism, the political arena, and the music industry. Jeffrey Fager, chairman of CBS News and executive producer of *60 Minutes*, gave the keynote address. The Hope and Stanley Adelstein Free Speech Essay Competition, conceived and underwritten by the club's beloved nonagenarians, invited students from area high schools to articulate a fresh perspective on free speech.

The celebration culminated in a gala at the Renaissance Cleveland Hotel, which drew over 950 members and guests and featured a panel of mostly local headliners who discussed "The Power of Ideas to Transform Communities."

In June 2013, after two decades as executive director of the City Club, Jim Foster retired. He received a warm sendoff at an evening reception, during which he was surprised by a video of himself as a young Air National Guard pilot. Club trustees praised Foster's intellect, humility, and stewardship. Rick Taft paid affectionate tribute to Foster as "a free-speech impresario of the first water" whose "healthy ego . . . loves to see others stride to a great podium and does not need limelight for itself." Taking the podium, the self-effacing Foster confirmed what everyone already knew: "I prefer to be on the other side of the microphone." He shared a treasured memento: a child's artwork created after a family visit to the City Club bearing the message "Free speech is cool."

On May 1, 2013, Dan Moulthrop was named chief executive officer of the City Club. An East Coast native with degrees in English and journalism, Moulthrop moved to Greater Cleveland with his wife Dorothy, a Cleveland native, in 2005. He joined radio station WCPN (Cleveland's NPR station), where he produced and hosted a daily public affairs call-in show. While at WCPN, Moulthrop was invited to moderate the 2005 Cleveland mayoral primary debate

City Club Chief Executive Officer Dan Moulthrop, left, interviews Peter Baker, chief White House correspondent for the *New York Times* and author of *Days of Fire: Bush and Cheney in the White House,* November 8, 2013. THE CITY CLUB OF CLEVELAND

Carrie Miller, program director of the City Club, holds the microphone for Stanley Adelstein at a forum featuring Dr. Akram Boutros, President and CEO of MetroHealth, December 6, 2013. The question-and-answer period, which follows every City Club presentation, is sacrosanct and has been since the club's founding in 1912. THE CITY CLUB OF CLEVELAND

at the City Club. The encounter made a lasting impression, demonstrating, he said, "that Cleveland is small enough that you can make a difference." Before coming to the City Club, Moulthrop briefly served as "curator of conversation" for the Civic Commons, a grant-funded project he co-founded to create open-source social media for civic purposes.

In an interview, Moulthrop described the City Club as "an exciting place with an important mission. The City Club brings in the best speakers. There's a real opportunity to introduce the ideas they bring into local and regional conversations." To that end, he initiated a comprehensive online strategy and introduced social media, offering a free lunch to those willing to tweet live from the forum and revamping the e-mail announcements of upcoming City Club programs to incorporate tweets for sharing with friends. He expected to get a little pushback—and he did. One longtime member responded archly, "I don't tweet and I never will." Another sniffed, "I assume I can still make a reservation by phone?" The old school needn't worry. "We recognize," Moulthrop said, "that we do have multiple audiences."

Moulthrop praised Jim Foster for reaching out to diverse audiences and for fostering an environment that, he said, "feels inclusive." He envisioned an opportunity to augment the club's aging and largely suburban membership by reaching out to new audiences, especially young professionals living and working downtown. It is a tall order: in 1988, the City Club counted 1,639 members; in 2013, just 793 (of which 70 were corporate).

Taking down a framed copy of the City Club creed from his wall, Moulthrop observed that it is as relevant today as when it was written in 1916. He expressed appreciation for the club's vibrant history and for the devotion of its stalwarts, both living and deceased. As exemplars he cited Stanley Adelstein, whose yeoman efforts to enlarge the Forum Foundation did much to protect the club's future;

and Ralph Hayes, the club's first paid secretary and the author of its creed, whose charitable trust has sent the club a check for $1,000 every year since his death in 1977.

In 1912, the club's founders enunciated a bold but simple premise: the City Club of Cleveland would be a "social club with a civic purpose." A century later, the City Club had fulfilled that vision—and moved beyond it.

Traditions once integral to its life as a private men's club—the partisan luncheon tables, the fraternal bonhomie, the annual skewering of local politicians in a staged satirical revue—over the years receded in importance. The commitment to free and fair speech became central. And as America struggled with the issues of race and gender, examining them against the principles on which this nation was founded, the City Club welcomed those debates to its podium—and listened.

The club found cause to examine its own policies and practices, both explicit (gender bias) and de facto (racial makeup), in the light of its professed ideals. It opened its doors to women and removed impediments to attendance and membership. As it had from the beginning, it continued to welcome vibrant, open discussion of the day's issues. Now, however, those discussions, absent the barriers incompatible with a changing world, occurred in an atmosphere of diversity and inclusion.

Meanwhile, the digital media revolution broke still other barriers, enabling the City Club, as it turned 100, to reach new audiences and communicate in ways that its founders could never have imagined. The club of Daniel Morgan, Newton D. Baker, and Peter Witt had become more than a social club with a civic purpose. It had become a national model of civic engagement and civil discourse, a place where the First Amendment was honored—and exercised—week after week. With vigilance, the City Club of Cleveland would retain the badge it had long claimed for itself as a Citadel of Free Speech.

> The club of Daniel Morgan, Newton D. Baker, and Peter Witt had become more than a social club with a civic purpose. It had become a national model of civic engagement and civil discourse, a place where the First Amendment was honored—and exercised—week after week.

On January 21, 2005, shortly after taking the
helm as CEO and president of the Cleveland
Clinic, Dr. Delos "Toby" Cosgrove told a City
Club audience that supporting local schools
will be the Clinic's No. 1 charitable activity. THE
CITY CLUB OF CLEVELAND

Part Two
# The Forum

# Memorable Speeches, 1987–2012

The forum is the heart and soul of the City Club. Each Friday, club members and guests convene for lunch, followed by a presentation by a speaker and a question-and-answer period. The latter is often lively, and always unscripted; anyone may raise a hand and ask a question. As *Washington Post* columnist David S. Broder observed from the City Club podium in 2000, "The fun and games begin when the speaker shuts up."

Since the club's founding in 1912, more than six thousand speakers—the famous and the not so well known in every field of human endeavor—have appeared at the City Club Forum. Asked to explain its value, club members point to the importance of civil discourse in an often uncivil society, and to the forum's role as an educational institution. One member says the best part of the weekly forum is "standing in the lobby [afterward], arguing points made in the speech." Still another savors the recollection of remarkable speakers whose "voices echo for years." (Twenty-two years later, this member vividly recalls Ramsey Clark's observation that "the first casualty of war is civil liberty.")

In 1929, in a small eponymous magazine, the printer and City Club member William Feather described the club as "a sanctuary where any idea can get a hearing, provided it is presented intelligently." On the Q & A that follows every speech, he observed: "A tradition requires that the speaker submit to questions from the floor. This period is lively and entertaining and occasionally brutal."

While civility is observed, few punches are pulled. Many a speaker has suddenly found him- or herself pressed to defend bold assertions or sweeping generalizations in the light of overlooked facts. Occasionally sparks fly. Flawed thinking is exposed. Bursts of eloquence or humor light up the room. The spectacle of quick thinking, an ungainly fumble, an agile recovery, can be as satisfying as any hotly contested playoff game or an evening of live theater.

In an era of virtual encounters and canned presentations, and media that increasingly pander to our prejudices and comfortable beliefs, the unfettered, face-to-face exchange of ideas remains central to the City Club's enduring appeal. For one hundred years, the club's weekly forum has brought to life the issues of the day.

The pages that follow recall and distill some of the most memorable City Club Forums from 1987 through 2012, the year of the club's centennial. This twenty-six-year period complements the period covered by a previous volume, *America's Soapbox: Seventy-five Years of Free Speaking at the City Club of Cleveland*, published in connection with the City Club's 75th anniversary in 1987.

The forums highlighted here were chosen by members of the club's Centennial Book Committee (its members are named in the Acknowledgements), who strove to present diverse voices and subjects. For each calendar year there is an extended profile of a leading forum speech followed by a sampling of other notable speakers who appeared that year. Taken together, these selections portray the panoramic drama to be found at the City Club Forum.

City Club President Richard Pogue congratulates Louis Stokes on the occasion of his induction into the City Club Hall of Fame, June 30, 1999. Stokes, whose brother Carl B. Stokes served as mayor of Cleveland from 1968 to 1971, joined the City Club in 1965 and regularly appeared at its podium during his long service in the U.S. House of Representatives. Following the presentation, the liberal Democrat delivered a blistering critique of the Congress from which he had retired six months earlier. An account of his speech appears on pages 106–7.

## Justice Sandra Day O'Connor
February 10, 1987

"I never aspired to be on the Court," Justice Sandra Day O'Connor told the City Club.

During his presidential campaign in 1980, Ronald Reagan pledged to appoint the first woman to the Supreme Court. On July 6, 1981, President Reagan telephoned O'Connor—then serving on the Arizona State Court of Appeals—to tell her she was his nominee to replace the retiring Potter Stewart. Notwithstanding the opposition of pro-life groups, which suspected that she would be unwilling to overturn *Roe v. Wade*, O'Connor was confirmed by the U.S. Senate by a vote of 99–0 and sworn in on September 25, 1981.

Direct and plainspoken, O'Connor hewed to her prepared remarks on "The Workings of the United States Supreme Court," delivering a primer of sorts. The Court's primary role is to develop a uniform and consistent body of law; it is an "unwritten rule" that four of the nine justices must accept a case for review; the justices meet once a week to discuss cases and discuss a case only once. O'Connor described the atmosphere of the Court as one of "warmth, kindness, and civility . . . of respect and even affection."

During the question-and-answer period, O'Connor further elucidated the workings of the nation's highest court while steering clear of political minefields. She politely declined to engage a gentleman who asked, "When does life begin? When does life end?" When another audience member criticized Attorney General Edwin Meese for making disparaging comments about Miranda rights (the mandatory warning given by police to a criminal suspect advising of the constitutional right against self-incrimination and of the right to have a lawyer present during any interrogation), O'Connor diplomatically told him that the president appoints a solicitor general, who represents him and the attorney general before the Supreme Court and may petition the Court for review.

> **"The Constitution is an enduring, remarkable, indeed an inspired document, very much alive, very healthy, and very much in use today."**

While the Supreme Court's position on a federal issue governs when that same issue arises in any other court of the land, O'Connor emphasized that the Court itself has no means of enforcing its decisions. Thus, following the Court's 1954 ruling in *Brown v. Board of Education*, in which it declared state laws establishing separate public schools for black and white students unconstitutional, President Dwight D. Eisenhower "actually had to call out federal troops to enforce the ruling." Sometimes enforcement follows readily. Following the Court's ruling in *Gideon v. Wainwright* (1963), in which the Supreme Court ruled that anyone too poor to hire a lawyer must be provided one free in any criminal case involving a felony charge, the state of Florida, the defendant in the case, immediately established a public defender's office.

O'Connor said the Supreme Court takes about 150 cases each year for plenary review, although it reviews some 4,000 cases a year from state supreme courts and the 13 federal appeals courts. The Court, in her view, is operating at maximum capacity.

Is there a pecking order among the justices? O'Connor was asked. "Oh yes, and I've just graduated," she said, expressing gratitude, even a touch of glee, that Antonin Scalia, appointed by President Reagan in 1986, had taken her place as the junior member, who must sit by the door during judicial conferences to carry messages in and out of the room and is the last member to walk into the court.

Asked to comment on the vitality of the 200-year-old Constitution, O'Connor said, "The Constitution is an enduring, remarkable, indeed an inspired document, very much alive, very healthy, and very much in use today."

JANUARY 30          MAY 22

### Dr. Mervyn Silverman

Dr. Mervyn Silverman,
president of the American
Foundation for AIDS
Research, said the lack of
a national policy on AIDS
was a disgrace. Calling
AIDS victims "modern-day
lepers," he said that society's
reaction to the disease—
bigotry, ignorance, denial,
anxiety, and scapegoating—
is as dangerous as the
disease, and the only
preventative medicine for
both is education.

### Thomas E. Wagner

Thomas E. Wagner, director
of the Edison Animal
Biotechnology Center at
Ohio University, said fear
of genetic engineering was
unwarranted. He described
altering the genetic codes of
cells in mice, making some
of them as large as rabbits,
and said such technology led
to a deeper understanding
of life's processes.

JULY 24

**Bayard Rustin**
Civil rights leader
Bayard Rustin contended
that automation and
technological advances
have left "economic
untouchables" in their wake:
poor blacks with nothing
but "muscle power" to sell,
whose inability to find work
"is far more devastating . . .
than racism ever will be."

**David Brower**, pioneer
environmentalist and
founder of Earth Island
Institute

**Ray Hodgson**, mayor of
Bluefields, Nicaragua

**Cesar Chavez**, co-founder
of the National Farm
Workers Association (later
the United Farm Workers
union, UFW), whose
aggressive but nonviolent
tactics made the farm
workers' struggle a moral
cause with nationwide
support

women's rights leader
**Eleanor Smeal**

# 1988

## President Ronald Reagan
January 11, 1988

Every president of the United States has an open invitation to address the City Club of Cleveland. President Ronald Reagan was the first sitting president to do so. Once arrangements had been made with the Stouffer Tower City Plaza Hotel to host the luncheon speech, all 1,200 tickets for the historic event were sold within the space of two hours.

Introducing the president, club Vice President Bruce Akers noted the City Club's recent 75th anniversary celebration and said, "We reach a high-water mark today." He also affirmed that, in keeping with City Club tradition, "there will be no pre-screened questions for the president."[1] The remark prompted President Reagan to quip, when he took the podium, "I've been assured that Sam Donaldson [the aggressive ABC News White House correspondent] is *not* a member of the City Club."

It was the quintessential Reagan—sunny and affable—who delivered an upbeat assessment of the U.S. economy, contrasting it with the "rampant inflation" and "erosion of investment and confidence" that characterized the previous decade. He cited a "return to free enterprise" and listed his administration's achievements: "We deregulated the economy, we cut taxes, and

we created 14.5 million new jobs. Employment, including employment of blacks, is at record highs."

The president highlighted the dramatic technological changes under way, saying, "We're not merely accelerating the processes of the Industrial Revolution; we're fundamentally transforming them." Through the miracle of the silicon chip, he said, productivity is exploding. With the global economy, "We are transcending [the limitations of] our natural resources," and with free trade, national boundaries are "becoming obsolete."

While admitting that the ballooning national deficit "is an embarrassment and a shame," the president contended that it was not caused by cutting taxes. Instead, he pointed the finger at Congress, saying, "It is time to fix the busted budget process." Reagan called for a line-item veto that would allow the president to eliminate "unwarranted appendages"—i.e., pork—in

budget bills. "No president," he said, "should be faced with an all-or-nothing budget."

Following the speech, the first question raised the subject of the Iran-Contra affair. Did anyone within the administration act outside the law? And, was he planning to pardon anyone who was involved in Iran-Contra? Without flinching, the president replied, "I did not see any law-breaking," while admitting that there were "individuals who did not keep me informed about what was going on." It was too early, he said, to talk about pardons.

Referencing the decline of the dollar and the October 1987 stock market crash, another audience member asked Reagan if there would be a recession. Pointing to "sixty-two months of expansion," the president said he doubted that the signs of recession are there—unless "doom-criers scare the people into one."

Another questioner quoted the president's own task force on the October 1987 stock market crash, which called the federal deficit "the unwanted and unpleasant stepchild of Reaganomics." Again the president pinned the blame on Congress, saying, "I haven't had a budget since I got here—only a series of continuing resolutions."

1. Those wishing to ask a question had submitted their names on cards and eight cards were drawn at random prior to the speech.

**Other notable speakers in 1988**

SEPTEMBER 14

OCTOBER 4

OCTOBER 7

### Ron Paul

Libertarian Party presidential candidate Ron Paul hammered the economic policies of the Reagan administration. "President Reagan made our country and people feel good about ourselves," he said, "[but] the nation is living beyond its means." He dismissed his campaign opponents, George Bush and Michael Dukakis, as "two big-government types."

### William J. Davis

William J. Davis, a Jesuit priest and a founder and principal investigator for the Christic Institute, a public interest law firm, discussed the firm's high-profile case, *Avirgan v. Hull*, filed on behalf of two journalists wounded in the 1985 La Penca bombing of a press conference being held by Contra leader Edén Pastora. The suit was filed against more than two dozen individuals, some of whom were to emerge as figures in the Iran-Contra affair.

### Zbigniew Brzezinski

Zbigniew Brzezinski, national security adviser under President Jimmy Carter, explained why he abandoned his longtime Democratic ties to support presidential candidate George Bush. "I happen to think, in the months and years to come, George Bush could work more effectively on a level of bipartisanship than Governor [Michael] Dukakis," he said, while also expressing concern that, under Dukakis's soft defense policy, the United States would not be able to negotiate from a position of strength in nuclear arms talks.

NOVEMBER 4          DECEMBER 9

### Gov. John Sununu

With fewer than 100 hours until the election, Republican Governor John Sununu of New Hampshire appeared at the City Club podium as a surrogate for George Bush, attacking Michael S. Dukakis's record as governor of Massachusetts. Owing to a communication breakdown within the Dukakis campaign, no one spoke on behalf of the Massachusetts governor, leading *Cleveland Plain Dealer* reporter Harry Stainer to write, "The free air time will be a campaign windfall for George Bush."

### Henry E. Hampton

Henry E. Hampton, producer of the acclaimed six-part PBS documentary *Eyes on the Prize*, observed that the dismantling of segregation between 1954 and 1965—"an eye blink of time"—changed the character of the country, giving rise to the women's movement and stoking opposition to the war in Vietnam.

**Larry Pacifico**, former world champion power lifter

**Michael Harrington**, co-chairman of the Democratic Socialists of America whose book, *The Other America*, helped to inspire the federal government's War on Poverty

environmental lawyer and advocate **Gus Speth**, co-founder of the Natural Resources Defense Council

**Dr. Toaru Ishiyama**, Japanese-American internee during World War II

**Harold John Russell**, chairman of the President's Commission on Employment of the Handicapped, who lost both hands in World War II and went on to win the Academy Award for Best Supporting Actor in 1947 for his role as Parrish in *The Best Years of Our Lives*

## Pei Min Xin
June 9, 1989

Five days after the Chinese government used tanks and armed soldiers to crush student-led pro-democracy protests in Beijing's Tiananmen Square, Pei Min Xin spoke at the City Club. The teaching fellow and doctoral candidate at Harvard University began his talk with a moment of silence for those killed or wounded.

Pei, a native of Shanghai, laid out the historical context of the protests. Following the "disaster" of the Cultural Revolution, he said, China's economy was in chaos, its people demoralized. Deng Xiaoping, the reformist leader of the Communist Party of China, led the nation toward economic reform, but there had been no political reform. Corrupt party officials continued to enrich themselves, many amassing fortunes through behavior Pei called "unacceptable to the people." Once China opened its door to the West, he said, "The bankruptcy of the Communist dictatorship became much more obvious."

Pei described the timeline of the protests. "At the beginning, students were making very minimal demands," he said. They had gathered in Tiananmen Square to mourn the death, on April 15, of Hu Yaobang, a liberal reformer who had been deposed after losing a power struggle with hardliners. They asked the government to reassess its policy toward peaceful protest, which the demonstrators viewed as a "patriotic act."

## I have vowed never again to serve a dictatorship.

On April 26, the government issued a warning to the protesters, charging them with "destabilizing the government." Later, two hundred students embarked on a hunger strike, demanding a dialogue with the government. Pei emphasized the "enormous support" for the student-led movement by the citizens of Beijing, putting the size of the pro-democracy demonstrations, at one point, as high as a million people.

On May 20, the government imposed martial law and began to mass thousands of troops around the square. The army, Pei said, "was not told about the people's peaceful demonstrations." Instead, the government branded them as "counter-revolutionaries."

In the early hours of June 4, the streetlights were extinguished and the protesters were herded toward a single exit. Troops armed with truncheons moved in and began beating those at the rear of the exiting crowd. Some began to bayonet the injured; others assaulted those attempting to offer assistance. The tanks rolled in.

**"American leaders should listen to the voices of the people, rather than to the voices of the dictators."**

In the days after the massacre, student leaders, union leaders, and intellectuals were arrested. "How many, we don't know," Pei said, calling on President George Bush to impose further sanctions. "A peaceful movement will grow violent," Pei predicted. "China is headed for chaos."

In response to a question, Pei said that Chinese students in the United States had been elated to see the peaceful protests at home. As to his future, he said, "I have vowed never again to serve a dictatorship." Acknowledging that sanctions will hurt ordinary Chinese citizens, Pei said, "People are willing to endure such hardships necessary for overthrowing this dictatorship." He drew applause when he added, "American leaders should listen to the voices of the people, rather than to the voices of the dictators."

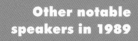

CITY CLUB VIDEO

FEBRUARY 10

APRIL 25

AUGUST 25

DEBATE

### Dr. Robert J. White
### Ingrid E. Newkirk

A debate on the subject of animals in medical research pitted Dr. Robert J. White, a renowned neurosurgeon who has experimented with monkey head and brain transplants, against Ingrid E. Newkirk, co-founder and president of People for the Ethical Treatment of Animals. White said animal research was essential to the study of diseases yet to be cured, including AIDS, Alzheimer's, and cancer. Newkirk posited that using animals for research is cruel and unnecessary, saying, "The bottom line is this: at one time it was legal to oppress women, but wasn't right. It was legal to intern Japanese-Americans, but wasn't right. It was legal to enslave human beings, but wasn't right."

### Dr. Alice Stewart

Dr. Alice Stewart, a British physician who discovered in the 1950s that X-rays of pregnant women could later cause their children to develop cancer, said more research needs to be done to assess the cumulative dangers of low-level radiation from all sources, including nuclear power and nuclear weapons plants. The U.S. Department of Energy, she charged, has denied access to its records, because it is "afraid of the truth."

### John Firor

The earth is becoming hotter, John Firor of the National Center for Atmospheric Research in Boulder, Colorado, warned. He explained that carbon dioxide, released into the air by automobiles and the burning of coal, trapped the sun's heat, causing a phenomenon known as the "greenhouse effect."

SEPTEMBER 15

OCTOBER 20

### Ohio Senator Michael R. White

In a jam-packed City Club mayoral debate among five primary candidates, Ohio Senator Michael R. White won thunderous applause with his call for better public safety, housing, education, and race relations. White's repeated mantra—"Continuity won't do"—was aimed at Council President George L. Forbes, the presumed frontrunner.

### Paul M. Kennedy

Yale historian Paul M. Kennedy, author of *The Rise and Fall of the Great Powers*, said the United States government should invest more money in long-term business, educational, and scientific research and less in the military to better compete with other economic powers. He said government-supported business investment should produce industry and jobs, not higher incomes for corporate executives.

**Rep. Patricia Shroeder**, Democrat of Colorado

**Thomas R. Donahue**, secretary-treasurer of the AFL-CIO and one of the most influential leaders of the post-World War II American trade union movement

**Leon Dash**, award-winning journalist and a founder of the National Association of Black Journalists

**Mary Lowe Good**, an inorganic chemist serving on the President's Council of Advisors on Science and Technology

Cleveland newspaper columnist and television personality **Dick Feagler**

**69**

## William Sloane Coffin
May 4, 1990

To achieve global security, "the world as a whole has to be managed, not just its parts," said the Reverend William Sloane Coffin. The former chaplain of Yale University, who resigned his ministry at New York's influential Riverside Church to pursue nuclear disarmament full time as the president of SANE/FREEZE, singled out three principal threats to global security: genocidal weapons, environmental degradation, and poverty. These, he said, "respect no human-drawn borders."

Coffin called "absolute national sovereignty" an impediment to global well-being. "There simply can be no lasting peace as long as nations jealously guard their sovereignty, each in pursuit of its own ends, subservient to no higher authority than its own," he said, calling instead for "one world" solutions.

"Imagination is more important than knowledge," Coffin declared. He called on his audience to imagine a world policed by peacekeepers stronger than any national force; a world where the money devoted to weapons

**"We can't imagine a world free of conflict, but we can imagine a world free . . . of violent conflict, of nuclear weapons, and of toxic waste."**

research is devoted instead to alternative energy research. "We can't imagine a world free of conflict," he said, "but we can imagine a world free . . . of violent conflict, of nuclear weapons, and of toxic waste."

Coffin asserted, "We don't need first-strike weapons. That's improving something that never should have been invented in the first place." With a military budget of $305 billion, "we are only aiding and abetting proliferation by not reducing [weapons] ourselves." With the end of the Cold War, he said of the continuing American military presence in Germany, we are reduced to defending "Western Europe from Eastern European shoppers."

On the subject of the environment, Coffin said that acid rain created in Great Britain poisons the waters of Scandinavia, and DDT sprayed in Central America has been found in the Great Lakes. Thus, he sermonized, "an ancient prophetic vision—human unity—today is a pragmatic necessity. We have to be meek or there won't be any earth to inherit."

Coffin concluded his speech with this plea: "All of us should pledge allegiance to the earth, and to the flora, fauna, and human life that it supports, one planet, indivisible, with safe air, water, and soil, [and] economic justice and peace for all."

In response to myriad questions from the audience, Coffin denounced genetic engineering, suggesting it might well be "our last evolutionary exam." Of the United Nations, he noted that the Soviets had paid their dues and asked "Why haven't we?" He contrasted American leaders today with those of our young nation, reeling off the names of Washington, Jefferson, Madison, Adams, and Franklin. But he held out hope that the "Cold War warriors" one day would be replaced by leaders with a more progressive agenda, adding, "To have hatred become a patriotic virtue is a terrible, terrible thing."

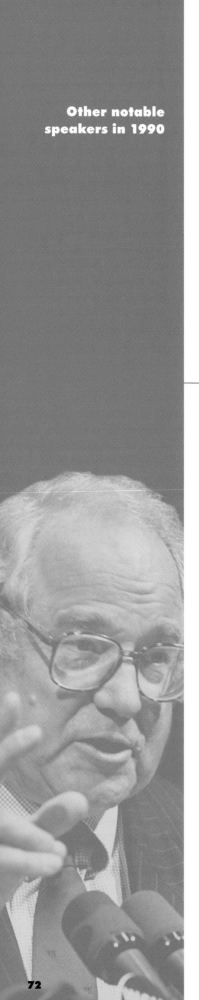

JANUARY 26

FEBRUARY 23

APRIL 7

### Christoph von Dohnányi

In a wide-ranging "conversation" between Thomas W. Morris, the executive director of the Cleveland Orchestra, and its music director, Christoph von Dohnányi, Dohnányi said that the orchestra should "integrate itself more into the community," paying special attention to attracting minorities. Comparing European and American attitudes toward culture, Dohnányi said the American attitude is often "Do we need this?" which he countered by asking, "Do we need flowers? Do we need books? Do we need love?"

### Taylor Branch

Taylor Branch, author of *Parting the Waters: America in the King Years, 1954–63*, said more writers should use oral history to prevent mythology from obscuring the truth of social movements before memories fade. Oral history is "history on the human level. You feel what it was really like."

### Solly Simalane

Economic sanctions against South Africa should be stepped up to force an end to apartheid, said Solly Simalane, a spokesman for the African National Congress. "Apartheid must be uprooted, root and branch."

CITY CLUB VIDEO

MAY 30

AUGUST 24

DECEMBER 7

### Dennis Barrie

Dennis Barrie, director of Cincinnati's Contemporary Art Center, addressed the City Club in the wake of concerted efforts by right-wing groups to shut down an exhibit of photographs by the late Robert Mapplethorpe on obscenity charges. The charges were still pending when Barrie spoke on the subject "Free Expression: The First Amendment and Robert Mapplethorpe," saying, "Our basic freedoms are at stake here."

### Maggie Kuhn

The national president of the Gray Panthers, 85-year-old Maggie Kuhn, said she has no use for retirement communities. "The separation of ages is not good for the aged and not good for society," she said. "Old people who isolate themselves cut themselves off from influencing the future."

### Harold A. Poling

Harold A. Poling, chairman and chief executive officer of the Ford Motor Company, said the economy is in a recession and that temporary layoffs of Ford employees would likely continue into the early part of 1991. Poling said he was "keeping a watchful eye on the events in the Middle East." Barring a war with Iraq, the economic downturn would be "relatively mild."

**Randall Hayes**, co-founder of the Rainforest Action Network

**John Glenn**, astronaut and U.S. senator from Ohio

**Paul Wolfowitz**, undersecretary of defense for policy in the George H. W. Bush administration

actress **Marlo Thomas**

**Lester Thurow**
November 1, 1991

"Build a better mousetrap," the saying goes, "and the world will beat a path to your door." Not in the twenty-first century, said Lester Thurow, dean of the Sloan School of Management at the Massachusetts Institute of Technology. Thurow, introduced to the City Club audience as an "intense, high-powered thinker" with a lust for mountain climbing, spoke on the subject "Economic Endgame for the Twentieth Century and Opening Moves for the Twenty-First."

"We are at a genuine historical turning point," Thurow declared. In the nineteenth century, Great Britain stood preeminent as an economic power because it had invented the steam engine, the spinning jenny, and the Bessemer furnace, and because of its proximity to abundant coal. In the twentieth century, America led the world because of another "invention": universal public education, an economic advantage that it enjoyed fifty to one hundred years before the other nations of the world.

"Profound revolutions in technology require profound revolutions in our society."

> **"[Ronald] Reagan persuaded every politician that optimists beat pessimists in America. But in so doing he changed the definition of optimist to someone who denies [we] have any problems."**

In today's global economy, the United States is behind the eight ball, misallocating our research and development spending, and underinvesting in education and workforce development.

The Japanese, Thurow said, devote two-thirds of their research and development spending to process engineering and one-third to new product engineering. American companies do the opposite. In the last fifteen to twenty years, we invented the video camera, the video recorder, and the fax machine. Who enjoyed the profits from such products? The Japanese—who manufactured them. "Not one person [in the United States] has earned their living making home video cameras—despite the fact that it was invented here."

In the global economy, Thurow said, "There are going to be low-tech products and high-tech products, but every product is going to be made with a high-tech process." And process technologies, so critical to our economy, require better education.

Thurow cited the case of 64-bit chips, which Motorola will make in Kyushu, Japan, where wages are *higher* than they are in the Silicon Valley. Motorola is going to Kyushu, he said, for an educated workforce that it cannot get here in the United States.

"Profound revolutions in technology require profound revolutions in our society," Thurow said. "In America we spend very little on the average worker. Ask someone in an American company, Who is the second-most important person in your company? They'll likely answer, the CFO. Ask the same question of someone working in a Japanese company, and they will point to the chief of human resources. That person is in the business of *workforce development*—not just administering pensions and benefits."

"In the twenty-first century, natural resources are irrelevant, capital moves around the world, new product technology moves around the world," Thurow said. "The only long-run competitive weapon is the quality of your workforce. You either play that game or you lose."

So how do we get from here to there? The Germans, Thurow said, copied our education system and made it better. Students attend school 250 days a year—not 180—and the school day is two hours longer. Our handicap is an ideological one: We consider the Founding Fathers gods and believe that the American system is perfect. He pointed the finger at "fifteen thousand school boards," few of which are succeeding, and asked, "Who in America can stand up and say, 'Let's get rid of local school boards'? It's un-American."

In response to a question from the audience, Thurow elaborated on this last point. "[Ronald] Reagan persuaded every politician that optimists beat pessimists in America. But in so doing he changed the definition of optimist to someone who denies [we] have any problems. In the old days, an optimist was someone who said, 'Hey, we've got a problem, but I've got a solution.' Today's presidential handlers would tell John F. Kennedy, 'Don't give the Man on the Moon speech,' because the Man on the Moon speech required Kennedy to say that the Russians are ahead of us in space. We need leadership. Are we going to get it? I don't know."

OCTOBER 25

NOVEMBER 8

NOVEMBER 22

**Harrison Young**

Harrison Young, a division director with the Federal Deposit Insurance Corporation, said three or four U.S. banks are failing each year and the losses will likely continue through 1993. He expressed regret that the "rich tradition" of banking as an honorable profession and a means of serving communities was eroding.

**Oliver North**

Promoting his new book, *Under Fire: An American Story*, Oliver North, a former staff member of the National Security Council, complained bitterly of his treatment by Congress, the media, and peace activists (including those picketing on the sidewalk outside the club) over his role in the Iran-Contra scandal. North said that President Ronald Reagan—contrary to the president's own statements—was fully apprised of the arms-for-hostages deal with Iran, the proceeds of which were used, illegally, to arm the Contra rebels in Nicaragua.

**Evan J. Kemp Jr.**

Americans need to reach consensus on the meaning of affirmative action or else risk a continuing rift between minorities and whites, the chairman of the Equal Employment Opportunity Commission told the City Club. Saying that he interpreted affirmative action to mean equality of opportunity for all people, Evan J. Kemp Jr., who uses a wheelchair, said, "It is important that we succeed as Americans, not as African-Americans, Irish-Americans, disabled-Americans, Hispanic-Americans, Asian-Americans. Let's finally get rid of the hyphens."

DECEMBER 12

**Rev. Jesse L. Jackson**
Delivering the keynote
speech at a symposium in
celebration of the 200th
anniversary of the Bill
of Rights, the Reverend
Jesse L. Jackson called
for national health care,
affordable housing, and
jobs for the 34 million
Americans living in poverty.
He contrasted the savings-
and-loan-industry bailout,
expected to cost the federal
government $600 billion,
with President Bush's
dismissal of a $6 billion
extension of employment
benefits as a "budget
buster."

**Robert Guccione**, founder
and publisher of *Penthouse*
magazine

**Dick Cheney**, secretary of
defense

**Ramsey Clark**, former
United States attorney
general whose Coalition to
Stop U.S. Intervention in
the Middle East opposed
the U.S.-led Gulf War and
sanctions against Iraq

**George Gilder**, writer,
intellectual, and Republican
Party activist whose 1981
bestseller *Wealth and Poverty*
advanced a practical and
moral case for capitalism

# 1992

## Russell Means
December 11, 1992

> "We have no property rights, and without property ownership, there can be no economic development."

In a red shirt, his raven braids festooned with beads, his ruggedly handsome face framed by a large necklace, the barrel-chested Oglala Sioux cut a striking figure. He spoke without notes, at times mangling quotations he attempted to paraphrase. But Russell Means, a leader of the American Indian Movement, commanded the audience's attention and was rewarded with appreciative applause.

Means began with a short list of targets for criticism. An American economy that makes it necessary for both parents to work "to grab a piece of the American pie," thereby weakening families. President Bill Clinton's appointment of Lloyd Bentsen as treasury secretary—"the one man you can blame for the savings and loan crisis!" Gasoline price-fixing and the government's failure to enforce anti-trust laws. "When's the last time you saw a gas [price] war?"

Means asked for a show of hands. "Who can find Bosnia and Herzegovina on the map?" Numerous hands went up. His next question was met with nervous laughter. "Who can tell me where the Western Shoshone live?" No one could. His point made, Means jumped to the heart of his remarks: "The government," he said, "isn't going to be happy until every Indian is on welfare."

Means charged that Indians are not allowed to enter the American system of capitalism. "We have no property rights," he said, "and without property ownership, there can be no economic development." He defiantly proclaimed, "The United States of America cannot prove title to Nevada!" Means pointed to

a single valid treaty, in 1869, which allowed the transcontinental railroad to go through the state. Yet, he said, the Indians who live there must obtain permits [from the federal government] to graze their cattle.

As a young man, Means spent a number of years in Cleveland. The federal Bureau of Indian Affairs was attempting to resettle Native Americans in a handful of large cities. Means worked as an accountant and later founded and served as the first president of the Cleveland American Indian Center. In 1972, Means sued the Cleveland Indians baseball team for its use of the Chief Wahoo logo, saying it slandered and degraded American Indians. Means later became the national coordinator for the militant American Indian Movement, leading protests that brought attention to poverty and discrimination suffered by his people and demanding adherence to historic treaties. More recently, he tried his hand at acting with a principal role in the highly acclaimed *The Last of the Mohicans* (1992).

Means blasted the Bureau of Indian Affairs as a "colonial structure" that keeps Indians hobbled and dependent. He declared that the Second Amendment is being "gutted" and the First Amendment "is gone." "Your great country . . . is fast becoming one big Indian reservation. And I'm scared," he said, because "I want my people to be free—and they will not be until you are."

Means's speech was brief, leaving lots of time for questions to which his answers were succinct. What party do you identify with? Libertarian, Means answered. (In 1987, Means ran for president, seeking the Libertarian Party nomination, but lost to Ron Paul.)

**"Abolish the Bureau of Indian Affairs. Imagine if we had a Bureau of Jewish Affairs or [a Bureau] of African Affairs. *We have the right to fail.*"**

Why don't American Indians seek change at the ballot box? Means fingered a button at the end of one braid and read its message: "You can vote but you can't choose." He expressed disgust for "Dempublicans" and endorsed third-party politics as the route to change.

Your complaints are valid, one questioner said, but what do you *advocate*? To this Means was unequivocal: "Abolish the Bureau of Indian Affairs. Imagine if we had a Bureau of Jewish Affairs or [a Bureau] of African Affairs. *We have the right to fail*," he said. Means stated that 40 percent of America's natural resources are on Indian lands, adding, "We should be as rich as the Saudis." Instead, windfalls from gas and oil extraction go to large corporations.

What, asked one questioner, can we as individuals do? Means offered only one idea: contact Representative Louis Stokes. (Stokes, a Democrat and a City Club member, then served on the House Appropriations Committee.) The United States government, Means said, needs to come to "an accommodation" with its native peoples.

Why can't Indian tribes be as successful as the Amish? Means's deadpan reply elicited laughter: "Because there is no Bureau of Amish Affairs."

Means concluded by expressing his desire to continue to work on freedom and independence for Indian people. "I want to see the first independent Indian nation in my lifetime," Means said. "There are 371 treaties signed by different Indian nations and the president of the United States. Every one of them has been violated."

JANUARY 6     FEBRUARY 28     MAY 1

### Rep. James Traficant

Representative James Traficant, Democrat of Youngstown, denounced the nation's two major political parties, saying that little separates them and that neither wants to make the painful decisions needed to help the ailing economy. The eccentric politician also apologized to "all hookers" for having once referred to members of Congress as "prostitutes."

### Caspar W. Weinberger

Caspar W. Weinberger, former secretary of defense and then publisher of *Forbes* magazine, said that the United States must help the former Soviet Union move to a free market economy to prevent the return of communism.

### Michelangelo Signorile

Michelangelo Signorile, a leading gay rights activist and journalist who pioneered the publication of the names of prominent gays (a practice known as *outing*), warned that gays and lesbians would someday explode in "outrageous activity" unless their demands for equality are heard.

CITY CLUB VIDEO

OCTOBER 2

OCTOBER 20

DECEMBER 29

**Louis Harris**

Veteran pollster Louis Harris warned against writing off Ross Perot owing to his late entry into the presidential race, saying that voters still had doubts about Governor Bill Clinton's character.

**DEBATE**

**Rep. Mary Rose Oakar**
**Martin Hoke**

A debate between Representative Mary Rose Oakar, an eight-term Democratic incumbent, and Republican Martin Hoke, a political novice, in the race for the new 10th Congressional District seat attracted national attention because it was so contentious. Hoke made Oakar's ethical lapses the central issue, while Oakar, wrote Mary Anne Sharkey, the politics editor of the *Cleveland Plain Dealer*, "turned sleazy politics into an art form" by dragging out personal issues.

**Butch Reynolds**

Butch Reynolds, who set a world record in the 400-meter dash in 1988 that stood for eleven years, gave a stirring account of the events that led to his successful lawsuit against the International Amateur Athletic Federation after a 1990 post-race blood test detected traces of a banned steroid, resulting in a two-year suspension.

Arkansas Governor and presidential candidate **Bill Clinton**

former governor of California and presidential candidate **Jerry Brown**

**Art Modell**, owner of the Cleveland Browns

**Lance Morrow**, senior writer, *Time* magazine

81

## Debate: Lieutenant Tracy Thorne vs. Major General J. Milnor Roberts

February 26, 1993

During his campaign for president in 1992, Governor Bill Clinton proposed an end to the military's exclusion of homosexuals. In May that year, Lieutenant Tracy Thorne openly identified himself as gay during an appearance on *Nightline*. The graduate of Vanderbilt University, who had graduated first in his flight training class and was serving in a jet squadron at Oceana Naval Air Station, was discharged from the military.

> **"Even the chairman of the joint chiefs, General Colin Powell, has said that there is no parallel between racial and homosexual discrimination."**

One month after the inauguration, as President Clinton weighed lifting the ban on gays in the military, Lieutenant Thorne, with his appeal pending, appeared at the City Club of Cleveland to debate retired Major General J. Milnor Roberts, a veteran of World War II and former Chief of Army Reserves, on "Homosexuality in the Military."

In his opening statement, Lieutenant Thorne drew a parallel between the military's discrimination against homosexuals and its historical discrimination against blacks. The United States and the United Kingdom, he said, are the only two members of NATO that do not allow homosexuals to serve in the military. He cited reports prepared for the Department of Defense as early as 1957 that said there was no reason to exclude homosexuals from the military. Regulations governing sexual behavior already exist, said the lieutenant, who dismissed the so-called "right to privacy"—often cited as a reason to exclude homosexuals—as nonsensical. "You would [think] that all the military does is take showers all day," he said, drawing laughter from the large audience. But Lieutenant Thorne was dead-serious when he subsequently said, "Don't tell me I can't serve my country because of your insecurities."

In his opening statement, General Roberts attributed President Clinton's proposal to end the ban on homosexuals in the military to either his lack of military experience or political payback. "Unfortunately," he said, "homosexuals have a tendency to be very promiscuous." He contended that "even the chairman of the joint chiefs, General Colin Powell, has said that there is no parallel between racial and homosexual discrimination." General Roberts cited the high medical costs associated with having homosexuals in the military. "Homosexuals have severe health problems," he said, including high incidences of AIDS, hepatitis, and "disorders of the anal-rectal region." Every veterans group opposes lifting the ban, he concluded, and the Department of Defense has said that admitting homosexuals "seriously impairs the accomplishment of the military mission."

In the Q & A, General Roberts was repeatedly challenged by members of the audience. In response to a question on the health statistics he cited, the general said they came from "the 1,500 homosexuals released from the service every year." Lieutenant Thorne countered that "AIDS is not a gay disease"—the single black male has the greatest incidence of AIDS—and advocated regular HIV testing of the armed forces. Thereafter, the exchanges grew impassioned and blunt.

When one man stood and read several passages in the Old Testament condemning homosexuality, Lieutenant Thorne responded by saying, "Let's not use the Bible to justify oppression any longer," drawing applause. General Roberts recounted the experience of his brother-in-law, who went to a military chaplain with a moral problem; as they knelt in prayer, he said, the chaplain "put a make on my brother-in-law."

What about men who abuse women in the military? General Roberts dismissed it as "normal boy-girl stuff" of a "different order" from homosexuality. Lieutenant Thorne countered: "[In some eyes] the label 'homosexual' makes me a predator. Sexuality is *not* immorality."

To those who say, "The military is not ready for change," Lieutenant Thorne stressed the military's need for guidance from civilians—"people who understand civil rights." Every now and then, he said, it needs a kick in the rear, and "it takes civilian leadership to do it."

General Roberts cited the recent Gulf War and growing tensions in the former Yugoslavia to underscore his contention that "lifting the ban on homosexuals will be prejudicial to the readiness of the forces." Lieutenant Thorne pointed to the high cost of discharging homosexuals and replacing them. In the 1980s, he said, 17,000 gays and lesbians were discharged. How many good people, he asked, simply left the military because they were tired of pretending to be someone they are not?

In his closing remarks, General Roberts again cited the "medical burden" imposed by homosexuals and insisted that the parallel between the historic unequal treatment of blacks and the present-day unequal treatment of homosexuals is invalid. "If President Clinton is not stopped from lifting the ban," he warned, "we may witness a shredding of the fibers of American society."

Lieutenant Thorne responded by saying that Roberts's arguments were based on stereotypes. "I am not a predator," he said. "I just want to do my job." Looking squarely into the eyes of his listeners, he said: "I am just like you. I'm the kid next door, I'm your son, I'm your daughter, your fireman, your policeman, your doctor, your lawyer. You've known us all along, but you've never really known us at all." He closed by quoting the words on the tombstone of Leonard Matlovich,[2] the first gay service member to purposely out himself to the military to fight its ban on gays: "They gave me a medal for killing two men and a discharge for loving one."

2. Air Force Sgt. Leonard P. Matlovich Jr. (1943–1988) was a Vietnam War veteran and recipient of the Purple Heart and the Bronze Star.

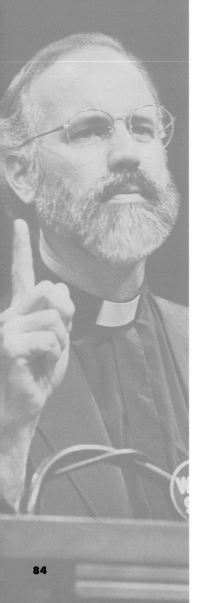

APRIL 2

MAY 7

MAY 14

**Boris Notkin**

On the eve of a summit meeting between Russian President Boris Yeltsin and President Bill Clinton, Boris Notkin, "Russia's Ted Koppel," spoke frankly about Russia's future prospects. The loyalties of the army and the KGB are unclear, he said, and poverty and corruption are growing. "There are so many question marks," he said, "you can know the answers only when the showdown comes." Notkin's program, *Good Evening Moscow,* is seen by forty million people each night.

**Michael Berenbaum**

Michael Berenbaum, project director for the Holocaust Museum in Washington, D.C., led the audience on a dramatic oral tour of the new museum, which records the murder of six million Jews. With genocide looming in Bosnia-Herzegovina, he said, President Bill Clinton has a tough decision to make.

**Father Gregory Boyle**

Father Gregory Boyle, the founder of Homeboy Industries, which provides training and support to formerly gang-involved and previously incarcerated men and women, said that youths join gangs out of despair and would drop gang activities if they were given jobs. Gangs today, said Boyle, a Jesuit priest, come from an urban underclass that appears permanent because the ladder of opportunity has been taken away. Police crackdowns only strengthen the resolve of gang members.

AUGUST 6

### Dr. Bernadine Healy

Dr. Bernadine Healy, former director of the National Institutes of Health, said the public should carefully scrutinize the Clinton administration's plans to overhaul health care. A Canadian-style health system, she said, "would cause a revolution" in the United States because "Americans are used to the best health care in the world," adding, "We don't want to do a massive social engineering that we [come to] regret."

**Stephanie Tubbs Jones**, Cuyahoga County prosecutor

**Owen Bieber**, national president of the United Auto Workers

**Dan Kiley**, an American landscape architect in the modernist style

**Senator Howard Metzenbaum**, Democrat from Ohio

**Rev. Joseph E. Lowery**, civil rights leader and former president of the Southern Christian Leadership Conference

## President Bill Clinton
October 24, 1994

One week before the mid-term elections of November 1994 that would deal Democrats a crushing setback by giving Republicans control of the House of Representatives for the first time in forty years, President Bill Clinton addressed the City Club. It was his third appearance before the club, and this time he came as a member. On his previous appearance as president, in 1993, Senator Howard Metzenbaum of Ohio had presented him with a gift membership. Clinton referenced the gift and warmly acknowledged the long-serving liberal Democrat, who was about to retire from the Senate. The consummate politician then recognized every officeholder in the room, singling out Cleveland Mayor Mike White with thanks for having met him at the airport at midnight. "He's leaving no stone unturned," Clinton remarked. "And here I thought that Cleveland already had every federal dollar that the law allowed!" The remark—vintage Clinton—drew hearty laughter from the large and largely Democratic audience.

Turning serious, Clinton gave an upbeat assessment of his economic program, which, he reminded the audience, had squeaked through Congress eighteen months earlier by a single vote in each chamber. "The mission," he said, "is clear: to empower the American people to compete and win." He ticked off his strategy: reduce the deficit; expand trade; increase investment

> **"No government can promise to protect people from global change. The changing nature of work requires more skills, and every American has to face these forces."**

in education and training; bring the benefits of free enterprise to our cities; and reinvent the federal government.

Clinton claimed credit for reducing a deficit that had "exploded in the 1980s" by reducing federal spending, including defense and discretionary spending, shrinking the federal work force, "reinventing government" through efficiencies implemented under the vice president, and procurement reforms aimed at eliminating "five-hundred-dollar hammers." From $305 billion two years ago, he said, the deficit has shrunk to $203 billion, and is projected next year to be $170 billion. Three years in a row of reduction, he said, has not been accomplished "since the Harry Truman administration."

"We are enjoying a period of economic expansion," the president declared. "We passed NAFTA (the North American Free Trade Agreement). Exports to Mexico are up 23 percent. America leads the world in the sale of autos for the first time since 1979, and auto workers in Detroit are complaining about overtime. We have opened new markets with Japan." America, the president declared, "is the most productive economy in the world."

Once the applause quieted, the president turned pensive, asking, "If all that is true, why aren't we happier?"

Clinton suggested a variety of factors, from the rancorous partisanship in Washington to the persistence of guns, drugs, and fractured families. Working people, he said, are losing their health insurance, and they are working harder to earn less. But, he cautioned, we need to resist quick fixes. "No government," he said, "can promise to protect people from global change. The changing nature of work requires more skills, and every American has to face these forces."

Turning briefly to the upcoming election, Clinton said that the "Contract with America" put forth by the Republicans "promises to explode the deficit" and is therefore "irresponsible."

"Other folks," he concluded, "see this as a pretty good country." Citing examples of America's leadership in the world, he finished by saying, "We need to build on that greatness."

In the question-and-answer period, the president was asked to expand on his criticisms of the "Contract with America." He said there were some elements he liked, but he disagreed with its call for a tax cut—"70 percent of the tax relief [will go] to upper-income people," he said—and with its proposal to "bring back Star Wars." "It doesn't add up," Clinton said. "It will increase the deficit and weaken the economy." He added, "The package is cynical because they won't say how they'll pay for it."

Another questioner wondered, "Why, with all the good things you're doing, don't we hear about them?" "It's a complicated thing," the president said. "I have to be a better communicator."

**Other notable speakers in 1994**

APRIL 1

JUNE 24

AUGUST 19

### Bud Selig

With the Cleveland Indians poised to unveil the team's new state-of-the-art baseball stadium, Bud Selig, acting commissioner of Major League Baseball, called Cleveland's turnaround part of a baseball renaissance. "When I got into the league there was no more troubled franchise in baseball than the Cleveland Indians. But what a great story that is now. It just goes to show what can happen when a baseball team and a community work together."

### Dr. M. Joycelyn Elders

Dr. M. Joycelyn Elders, who practiced as a pediatrician before being appointed as U.S. Surgeon General, implored a large City Club audience to make the county's children a higher priority. Elders said one in four children today is poor; for minority youth, that number is one in two. She cited the growing incidence of AIDS and HIV among teenagers and said that the United States has more teen pregnancies than any other industrialized nation.

### M. Cherif Bassiouni

M. Cherif Bassiouni, a legal scholar at DePaul University who headed up a U.N. commission on war crimes in the former Yugoslavia but was given no money and no mandate, said "Winners are not prosecuted for war crimes but, unfortunately, not even losers are being prosecuted for war crimes today." As examples, he pointed to Jean-Claude "Baby Doc" Duvalier of Haiti and Idi Amin of Uganda. Without justice for victims, grievances can re-escalate into war—just as they have in the Balkans, he said.

SEPTEMBER 27

### Gerry Adams

On a tour of U.S. cities to promote the peace process, Gerry Adams, the head of Sinn Fein, the political wing of the Irish Republican Army, attempted to project a fresh image as the statesman who can help lead Northern Ireland to peace. Evading questions about whether he was ever an active member of the IRA itself and consistently refusing to condemn the violence used by his compatriots, Adams confined his remarks to what he called an opportunity here and now for a political settlement. Was Adams, as widely believed, a commanding officer in the Belfast IRA in the early 1970s? Did he openly oppose the first major IRA ceasefire in 1975? "When you're in prison," he said, "you're out of it."

**Nicholas Lemann**, national correspondent, *The Atlantic Monthly*

**George Stephanopoulos**, senior adviser to President Bill Clinton

**Joan Dunlop**, women's health rights advocate

## House Speaker Newt Gingrich
July 31, 1995

Speaker Newt Gingrich appeared still to be savoring the previous year's elections, in which Republicans gained 54 seats and took control of the House of Representatives for the first time since 1954. Taking the podium before a capacity audience in the ballroom of the Stouffer Tower City Plaza Hotel in a city whose baseball team was in hot pursuit of a pennant, he declared: "I am an optimist. The last time there was a Republican Speaker of the House Cleveland was in the World Series!"

The onetime college teacher proceeded to deliver a lesson in "new thinking vs. old thinking" about public policy issues, first laying out the "planning and leadership model" being used by the House of Representatives. "We have to communicate a vision of a better twenty-first century," said Gingrich, "a vision of better jobs with better pay." He enumerated nine key strategies to achieve that vision.

Number one: Renew American civilization. The Declaration of Independence, Gingrich said, "granted each of us a right to the *pursuit* of happiness; it did not create a federal Department of Happiness." If we want to compete with Germany, Japan, and China, we need a stronger work ethic, and students need to do two hours of homework every night. Unemployment compensation should be tied to the attainment of education and job skills, "not used to subsidize your hunting and bass fishing."

We must compete in the world market, enter the information age, replace the welfare state with an opportunity state, decentralize power away from Washington, and take the downsized federal government that remains and "make it the best it can be." We have to balance the budget. In 1997, Gingrich predicted, interest on the federal debt will exceed the defense budget.

We must suppress violent crime and defeat the drug culture. "It turns out that Nancy Reagan was right," Gingrich said. "No one [today] is saying 'Don't do it.'" He called for the death penalty for drug dealers. "Right now . . . we give the 17-year-old with $500 worth of crack five years in jail, and the guy in the Learjet goes back to Switzerland with his millions. It's time the guy in the Learjet lost the jet and lost his life." Lastly, America must lead the planet. "We have to, because no one else can," Gingrich said.

The speaker closed his talk with a few words on Medicare. A Republican task force was then at work to produce an alternative to the present system. "I think you are going to be pleased," he said, adding that the Democrats are "going to say anything, do anything . . . to scare senior citizens."

Gingrich deftly disposed of questions from members of the audience selected by lottery. One questioner noted that GOPAC, a "527" organization (the reference is to a section of Internal Revenue Code) devoted to educating and electing a new generation of Republican leaders, has received $10 million in corporate contributions. What are you promising in return? he asked. "Better government," Gingrich replied, earning applause.

Asked about tort reform, the speaker said that the present litigation system "encourages us to fight with each other." He declared that "there are more lawyers in Georgia than in Japan. We ought to triple the number of scientists and halve the number of lawyers."

To a query about global competition, Gingrich called for a "revolution in education," saying that "26 percent of fourth graders cannot read at grade level." As a reward for learning to read, he said, every child should be given a laptop.

> "I am an optimist. The last time there was a Republican Speaker of the House Cleveland was in the World Series!"

"It turns out that Nancy Reagan was right. No one [today] is saying 'Don't do it.'"

One questioner brought up the mostly African American crowd of anti-Gingrich protesters outside the hotel, to which Gingrich replied, "We"—meaning the Republican Party—"are trying to reach out to everyone, of every background . . . No community has been more devastated by the drug culture than the African American community." He pointed to Ohio Secretary of State Ken Blackwell and Senator J. C. Watts of Oklahoma, both African Americans, as evidence of the party's inclusiveness.

What about tax relief for small business? Gingrich said the Kemp Commission on tax reform was working on it. His next line—"The battle cry 'Get the IRS out of [my] life' has a certain appeal"—drew hearty applause.

Gingrich refused to take the bait of one effusive admirer, who asked if the speaker might take this opportunity to announce his candidacy for president of the United States. "No, not today," he replied.

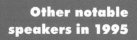

CITY CLUB VIDEO

MARCH 10      JULY 28      AUGUST 15

### Paul Hawken

The United States is on the verge of a new industrial age in which it will use fewer natural resources and more human resources, said Paul Hawken, an entrepreneur, environmentalist, and co-founder of Smith & Hawken. The new Republican-dominated Congress, he said, "represents not a sign of the future but an effort to hold back change."

### Ronald S. McNeil

Ronald S. McNeil, president of the American Indian College Fund and a descendant of the great Lakota chief Sitting Bull, said the fund uses the money it raises to support twenty-nine Indian colleges located on or near Indian reservations nationwide. Indian students have a higher success rate at Indian colleges, which offer classes in the context of native culture, than at standard colleges. McNeil said he objected to the logo of the Cleveland Indians baseball team but not to its name.

### Karen Horn

In the quest to trim the federal budget deficit, her primary target would be entitlements, said Karen Horn, chairman and chief executive of Bank One, Cleveland, who serves on the Bipartisan Commission on Entitlement and Tax Reform. We are living with promises that we cannot keep, Horn said of the social programs intended to help the poor and the elderly.

NOVEMBER 10

### Rev. Otis Moss Jr.

The Million Man March in Washington, D.C., was a "utopian moment" in the nation's civil rights history—"that moment when we stand in the midst of an ever-deepening crisis and taste the new future with fresh hope," said the Reverend Otis Moss Jr., pastor of Cleveland's Olivet Institutional Baptist Church. "It was about atonement," Moss said of the previous month's gathering, organized and led by Louis Farrakhan of the Nation of Islam, which called on black men to renew their commitments to their families and communities.

**Roberta Cooper Ramo**, the first woman to serve as president of the American Bar Association

**Jo Ann Davidson**, the first (and, to date, only) woman to serve as speaker of the Ohio House of Representatives

**Haley Barbour**, chair, Republican National Committee

**Bob Schieffer**, chief White House correspondent, CBS News

**Robert P. Bergman**, director of the Cleveland Museum of Art

## Gerda Weissmann Klein and Kurt Klein
November 15, 1996

Gerda Weissmann was fifteen in the autumn of 1939 when the Nazis marched into her village in Poland, near the Czech border. Her brother was taken away for conscription. Three years later, her parents were sent to Auschwitz, where they would perish; Gerda was sent to a succession of slave labor camps in Germany.

Researchers at the National Holocaust Memorial Museum have catalogued some 42,500 ghettos, slave labor sites, concentration camps, and extermination facilities set up throughout Europe by the Nazis during Hitler's reign of brutality, from 1933 to 1945. A dwindling number of survivors remain to provide personal testimony as did Holocaust survivor Gerda Weissmann Klein and her husband Kurt Klein in a grim yet uplifting talk.

Weissmann Klein, an author and humanitarian, assured the audience that she was not there to describe the horror of her experience. "It was not unique," she said quietly, "it happened to everyone." Instead, she told a remarkable story of survival, distilling it in these words: "My friends died without a crust of bread, and I am here."

In the winter of 1945, Weissmann Klein was part of a forced march to Czechoslovakia in response to the advance of the Allied forces. Of the 4,000 women who started out, she said, only 120 survived, the others succumbing to starvation, exposure, and arbitrary executions.

On May 7, 1945, with the U.S. Army approaching, the Germans locked their captives in an abandoned factory and, before departing, set explosives to blow it up. But a torrential rain prevented the explosives from detonating,

and Weissmann Klein saw a car marked with a white star coming toward the factory. To the soldier who approached from the car, she said, "I'm Jewish, you know." "So am I," Lieutenant Kurt Klein replied. The two were married a year later.

While "the miracle of liberation [could not] restore the past," Weissmann Klein said, she settled with her husband in Buffalo, New York—"the most beautiful city in the world"—where, gradually, "fear changed to cautious security, pain turned to joy, and death became life when our children were born."

Weissmann Klein, who recounted her wartime experiences in a memoir, *All But My Life* (1957), closed her talk by describing the view from her Cleveland hotel room the previous evening. As snow softly descended and the city lights came on, it reminded her of her snowy march during captivity, when, she said, "hungry, cold, tired, and lonely, I saw a house with a light on and imagined a woman preparing a meal for her family." That indelible image inspires her even today "to reflect on our freedom and bounty."

Kurt Klein took the podium to share his account. As a soldier with Patton's Third Army and with the end of the war in sight, he was advancing into Czechoslovakia. At Volary, his unit heard of a group of women locked in a factory. "What we found there," he said, "far exceeded anything the imagination can conjure up." Gerda led him inside, where he saw skeletal figures scattered around the floor, some lying on straw, many close to death. Gerda made a sweeping gesture with her hand and astonished him by reciting a line from Goethe: "Noble be man, merciful and good." Klein said, "Out of this scene sprang our relationship; and from the bitterness of war, something positive arose."

**"What we found [at the abandoned factory in Volary] far exceeded anything the imagination can conjure up."**

Kurt Klein said he felt an obligation to let the world know what happened, for even as we treat the Holocaust as a barbarism now behind us, fanaticism and intolerance continue. He cited the atrocities in Bosnia, Rwanda, and Oklahoma City. The Kleins then took questions from the rapt, even reverent audience.

Weissmann Klein was asked if she had experienced any kindness during her years of captivity. Yes, she said, from one policeman and one camp director. Did no others express understanding? On the death march through Germany "any who sought help from nearby farmhouses were turned over [to the Nazis]," she said, but once they had crossed the border into Czechoslovakia "the Czechs threw bread at us." She noted that her book, now a classic of Holocaust literature, has been published all over the world—"but never in Germany."

How did you sublimate your anger? "Anger and hatred are emotions you cannot afford if you want to build a new life," Weissmann Klein answered. What sort of people planned the facilities for the Holocaust? Kurt Klein replied that the Final Solution—the industrialized mass slaughter of the Jews—was planned by the Nazi hierarchy in 1942, but it was committed by "ordinary people. A whole cross-section of society did it, and did it gleefully."

CITY CLUB VIDEO

APRIL 19          JUNE 7          JULY 23

### Dr. Francis S. Collins

Mapping and identifying each of the 100,000 human genes to determine the exact sequence of the three billion nucleotides forming the building blocks of human DNA (deoxyribonucleic acid) "will have profound consequences for the human race," said Dr. Francis S. Collins. The director of the National Center for Human Genome Research cautioned that the ability to identify specific genes responsible for hereditary diseases holds ethical pitfalls as well as medical promises.

### John Sweeney

AFL-CIO President John Sweeney told an overflow audience that, since 1980, executive compensation is up 400 percent and corporate profits are up 200 percent. Meanwhile, workers are left to wonder how to pay for medical treatment without health care benefits. "America needs a raise," he said, and the AFL-CIO will work to revitalize the labor movement by organizing new members, particularly young, female, and minority workers.

### Robert Reich

With unemployment below 5 percent and no inflation in sight, Labor Secretary Robert Reich told a capacity crowd, "I believe we're on the right track." To Reich, the "right track" is a workforce that employers treat as an asset to be developed, not as a cost to be borne. "That way, your major resource is working for you, rather than against you."

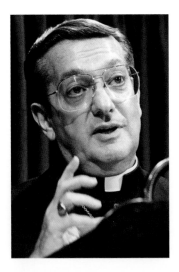

OCTOBER 22

**Bishop Anthony M. Pilla**
Cleveland Catholic Bishop
Anthony M. Pilla, president
of the National Conference
of Catholic Bishops, said
religious faith mandates a
concern for the city and its
people, and called on all
people to become advocates
for social justice in cities.
"We are all impoverished
when society fails to
incorporate into its political
and economic policies
measures to empower those
left out of the mainstream,"
he said.

**Sarah Brady**, wife of former
White House Press Secretary
James Brady and a leading
proponent of gun control

**A. Leon Higginbotham Jr.**,
African American civil rights
advocate, author, and federal
appeals court judge

**Janet Reno**, attorney general
of the United States

# 1997

## Rita Dove and Henry Louis Gates Jr.
May 9, 1997

This extraordinary City Club Forum featured two distinguished scholars: Henry Louis Gates Jr., chairman of the African American Studies Department and the W. E. B. Du Bois Professor of Humanities at Harvard University; and Rita Dove, the Commonwealth Professor of English at the University of Virginia and former poet laureate of the United States. Both served on the jury (Gates as chair) of the Anisfield-Wolf Book Awards and were in Cleveland to attend the previous evening's awards ceremony.

Gates introduced Dove, an Akron native and personal friend, with a long list of her accomplishments: recipient of a Fulbright Fellowship for study in Germany, writer-in-residence at Tuskegee University, recipient of a Pulitzer Prize for her collection *Thomas and Beulah*, and the first African American to be honored as poet laureate. Gates called her "a songstress with words" and a writer who "loves beauty as much as truth."

Dove began by reading "The Buckeye," a paean to a fruit deemed—as she writes—"so useless, so ugly" but

> in autumn
> when the spiny helmets split
>
> open,
> there was the bald
> seed with its wheat-
>
> colored eye.
> We loved
> the modest countenance beneath
>
> that leathery cap.

When she reads this poem, she said, people often ask, why do you get so excited about this little thing? "Poetry," Dove countered, "connects us with every person we have ever been or dreamed of being."

She next recited what she called "one of my more overtly political" poems. Titled "Parsley," it recalls the October 1937 massacre of 20,000 Haitians in the Dominican Republic by Rafael Trujillo, in which the brutal dictator ordered his troops to apply a shibboleth to distinguish immigrant Haitians from native Dominicans. They held up a sprig of parsley—*perejil* in Spanish; whether or not they rolled the "R" determined their fate. Dove read clearly, flawlessly, and fearlessly:

> El General
> searches for a word; he is all the world
> there is
>
> El General has found his word: *perejil*.
> Who says it, lives. He laughs, teeth shining

Her next poem, "My Mother Enters the Work Force," celebrates the woman who worked as a seamstress to put herself through the ABC Business School. It recounts her mother's perseverance

> until she could break a hundred words
> with no errors—ah, and then
>
> No more postponed groceries,
> and that blue pair of shoes!

**"It is important to master the King's English, not because it's something spoken at Buckingham Palace, but because it was something spoken by Martin Luther King. And that is the great tradition to which we all are heir."**

Following three short poems from her most recent book, *Mother Love* (1995), the poet closed with a selection from "Seven for Luck," a song cycle on which she was then collaborating with the composer John Williams. Gates then joined Dove at the podium to take questions.

One exchange stood out. Longtime City Club member Bob Lustig observed that over a period of more than thirty years he had witnessed speeches delivered by numerous African Americans, each of whom spoke clear American English. "Can one succeed without it?" he asked. Gates stepped in to respond.

"All Americans should speak fluently," he said, adding, "All Americans should [also] speak a second language." He continued: "The language of the marketplace is standard English. [You] can't get a job at I.B.M. or Microsoft talking about 'dis' and 'dat.'" At the same time, Gates said, he celebrates African American Vernacular English, which fills the first half of *The Norton Anthology of African American Literature* (1996) he recently co-edited. "We [blacks] have our own culture . . . but still we need to learn how to use the language of the marketplace—how to cross over, how to participate in the larger American society." His final point earned acclamation: "It is important to master the King's English," Gates said, "not because it's something spoken at Buckingham Palace, but because it was something spoken by Martin Luther King. And that is the great tradition to which we all are heir."

FEBRUARY 21

MAY 16

MAY 30

### Walter E. Massey

Society and science will benefit if more blacks become scientists, said Walter E. Massey, president of Morehouse College and former director of the National Science Foundation. "People from different backgrounds can bring different and unusual insights to the study of science," he said, "not necessarily because of their racial or cultural heritage, but because of their complete life experiences, among which their racial and cultural heritage is only a part."

### Fernando Remírez de Estenoz

Cuba's top diplomat in the United States, Fernando Remírez de Estenoz, told the City Club that the 36-year trade embargo has caused great problems for Cuba, hurting access to medicine, stopping the flow of machines and parts, and inflating the cost of virtually all goods Cuba imports from other countries. He said Cuba was in the midst of an economic modernization that requires foreign investments, but that Cuba will never sacrifice its sovereignty and self-determination. "We are sure that, in the future, Cuba and the U.S. will have normal relations, and that our children will face each other not with weapons, but only in the sports stadiums."

### Raul Yzaguirre

Raul Yzaguirre, president of the National Council of La Raza, the nation's largest Hispanic civil rights and advocacy organization, said the perception of Latinos as lazy and unpatriotic could not be further from the truth. Latinos, he said, "represent the best of American life—family, work, and patriotism." To understand Latinos, it is necessary to learn about the Spanish-American and Mexican Wars. "The legacy of colonialism and conquest is something people don't want to admit to," he said.

SEPTEMBER 12

### Diane Rehm

Diane Rehm, accustomed to asking the questions as host of *The Diane Rehm Show*, a nationally syndicated talk show on National Public Radio, had to answer them. Following her talk on "The Pervasive Influence of Media," she was asked about the acquisition of the major television networks by large corporations and its impact on network news. Rehm observed that health stories increasingly seem to lead the broadcasts, with foreign policy and congressional news trailing later if they are covered at all. "The cross between news and entertainment worries me," she said.

conductor and pianist
### Vladimir Ashkenazy

### Stuart J. Youngner,
professor of psychiatry, medicine, and biomedical ethics, Case Western Reserve University School of Medicine

### Millard Fuller, founder
and president of Habitat for Humanity International

## Marian Wright Edelman
October 3, 1998

"America is riding high and Wall Street is booming," Marian Wright Edelman told the City Club, "but extraordinary child needs persist, which jeopardize both our national soul and our social fabric."

For three decades, Marian Wright Edelman has been working to ensure that the youngest and most vulnerable members of society don't go without. After graduating from Spelman College and Yale Law School, Edelman went to the crucible of Mississippi in the early 1960s, where she became the first black woman admitted to the Mississippi bar and began practicing law with the NAACP Legal Defense and Educational Fund. After witnessing abject poverty up close, she took her outrage to Washington, D.C., where she founded the Children's Defense Fund in 1973 as a voice for poor, minority, and disabled children.

Edelman spelled out the problem in plain language. Over 14 million children—one in five—are poor. One million children are reported abused and neglected each year—one child every ten seconds. One and a half million children live with their grandparents. And, despite a booming economy, working families cannot earn wages high enough to lift their children out of poverty. "We have to change the debate," Edelman said. "We don't just need to end welfare as we know it; we've got to change child poverty as we know it."[3]

What can we do? Edelman offered six ideas.

1. We can commit—and recommit—ourselves to making our community better.

2. We can affirm and nurture each child's unique strengths.

3. We must counter the idols of our culture by teaching our children the difference between heroism and celebrity.

4. We must never lose hope, and we must give our children hope.

5. We must reach out to—and save—one child not our own.

6. We must be good parents and caregivers.

Edelman described a recent victory. "Who would have thought," she said, "that child advocates could put together the dream legislative team of the conservative Senator Orin Hatch of Utah and the liberal Senator Teddy Kennedy of Massachusetts, to get enacted a $48 billion bipartisan state child health insurance program partially funded by [the] tobacco tax—which everybody said wasn't possible?" Through that program, called Healthy Start, five million of the nation's poorest children will get health care.

Edelman praised Ohio as one of the first states to implement Healthy Start, but said that stepped-up outreach was still necessary so that those eligible for the program know about it. And it needs to be expanded to cover a greater number of poor children.

"We do not yet know the results of welfare reform," Edelman cautioned. By 2000, she said, 96,000 adults and 183,000 children stand to lose cash assistance, and it is critically important to have the necessary support systems in place—job training, quality child care, and transportation planning.

Edelman lamented the many perils poor children commonly face and reminded her audience of Senator Robert F. Kennedy's visit to Cleveland in April 1968, one day after the assassination of Martin Luther King Jr.,

3. On August 22, 1996, President Bill Clinton signed into law the Personal Responsibility and Work Opportunity Reconciliation Act of 1996, which added a workforce development component to welfare legislation, encouraging employment among the poor and fulfilling his 1992 campaign promise to "end welfare as we have come to know it."

**"We must counter the idols of our culture by teaching our children the difference between heroism and celebrity."**

when he spoke somberly of "the mindless menace of violence." In the thirty years since, she said, countless American men, women, and children "have been killed by guns in our nation's undeclared twentieth-century civil war." Pointing to poverty, the disintegration of the family, easy access to firearms, and "gangs of inner-city youths relegated to the cellar [of society]," she urged her listeners to "Vote for people who vote for children."

She closed with a prayer: "Oh God, forgive our rich nation that lets children be the poorest group of citizens . . . Oh God, forgive our nation that thinks security rests in missiles rather than in mothers, and in bombers rather than in babies . . . Help us never to confuse what is legal with what is just and right in your sight."

APRIL 17                    MAY 20                    JULY 31

### Susan E. Rice

Susan E. Rice, the U.S. government's top Africa policy official, surprised the City Club audience by naming Botswana, in southern Africa, as the world's fastest-growing economy and one of many little-known success stories on the continent. Rice, one of the youngest assistant secretaries of state in U.S. history, helped plan President Bill Clinton's recent six-nation trip to Africa, the most ambitious of any sitting president.

### Biljana Plavsic

Speaking through an interpreter, Biljana Plavsic, president of the Republika Srpska (Bosnian Serb Republic), said the Dayton Peace Accords of 1995 are not an ideal solution, but they are working. "This terrible war has left a bitter aftertaste in the mouths of all the peoples of Bosnia, which is why all three parties—Serbs, Croats, and Muslims—must work hard to overcome the legacy of hate . . . All parties must learn to recognize the humanity of their former enemies, and to give them opportunities to enjoy full democratic rights."

### Steven F. Goldstone

"Americans think smoking is worse for you than it is," said Steven F. Goldstone, citing a growing list of diseases that scientists cannot definitively trace back to the effects of smoking. The chairman and CEO of RJR Nabisco acknowledged that cigarettes are a "risky product" that contributes to health problems, but said the solution is to find a compromise that helps end under-age smoking but does not infringe on the rights of smokers. Goldstone spoke one month following the collapse of a senate bill that would have required tobacco companies to pay $516 billion over 25 years in addition to significantly curtailing the advertising of cigarettes.

DECEMBER 4

**Ben Cohen**

Ben Cohen, chairman of
Ben & Jerry's Ice Cream
and president of Business
Leaders for Sensible
Priorities, told the City
Club that the United States
could easily trim $40 billion
from defense spending
to fund unmet domestic
needs. "How can you look
a hungry kid in the face
who comes from a crime-
infested neighborhood with
disintegrating schools and
say we are sending excess
money to the Pentagon that
it didn't even ask for?"

**Dr. Thomas H. Murray**,
director of the Center for
Biomedical Ethics, Case
Western Reserve University

**Susan Taylor**, editor in
chief, *Essence* magazine

**Dr. Helen Caldicott**,
physician and anti-nuclear
activist

**Iris Chang**, author of
*The Rape of Nanking: The
Forgotten Holocaust of World
War II*

## Louis Stokes
June 30, 1999

Growing up in Cleveland in the 1930s and 40s, former Representative Louis Stokes said the only role models he had were Joe Louis, a boxer, and Bill "Bojangles" Robinson, a tap dancer. Then he learned of the appearance, at the City Club, of Adam Clayton Powell Jr., a militant civil rights leader and eloquent orator elected to Congress in 1944 to represent the congressional district that included New York's Harlem. Stokes looked to Powell as a role model. In 1968, when Stokes became the first African American elected to Congress from Ohio, Powell was still there. Over the next three decades, Stokes said, he served with some "legislative giants": Carl Albert, Tip O'Neill, Hale Boggs, Lindy Boggs, Claude Pepper, Moe Udall, Peter Rodino, Charles Vanik, Jim Wright, Martha Griffiths, and many others. "Those Congresses," Stokes said, "were much different from the Congresses today."

The current Congress, Stokes said, now entering its seventh month, has yet to enact any significant legislation. Since 1994, not a single piece of landmark legislation has been enacted. Most legislation, "such as it is," is enacted through the appropriations process, but even that is stymied. Stokes, who retired from Congress in January, didn't mince words—he no longer had to—pinning the blame on the conservative right of the Republican Party. "They were elected to Congress on anti-government platforms," he said. "Their dilemma is serving in a legislative body which exists for passing legislation, to which they are opposed, because their goal is to get the government out of the business of passing laws—which might not be a bad idea when you consider their action this past week in passing an amendment to post the Ten Commandments in schools as a remedy for violence in schools."

Stokes decried the "mean-spiritedness" that permeates Congress today, which, he said, "is antithetic to the history, precedents, and traditions of Congress." He singled out for criticism the "rancor, stridency, discord, and divisiveness" on display during the impeachment hearings of President Clinton. Meanwhile, he said, the nation awaits a solution to the long-term insolvency of Social Security and 43 million Americans who are without health insurance. The lack of productivity, said Stokes, helped him decide, after fifteen terms in Congress, "that my time and energy . . . could be better used elsewhere."

Stokes spoke at the Sheraton City Centre Hotel on the occasion of his induction into the City Club Hall of Fame, and the room was crowded with friends, family, and well-wishers. As a member of the City Club of Cleveland since 1965, Stokes has often appeared at its podium. During his tenure in Congress, no matter how solid his lead or anemic his opponent, he never failed to appear there for the traditional candidates' debate. Paraphrasing a quote attributed to Voltaire, Stokes said the City Club "keeps alive the old adage, 'I disagree with what you say, but I will defend unto death your right to say it.'"

Following a standing ovation, Stokes took questions.

On our nation's failure to pay its U.N. dues, Stokes said, "I'm on record: It's shameful; it's wrong." On the rancor in Congress, he warned that "the so-called religious right is a very dangerous group of people. Many of the things they espouse are a real threat to democracy." He denounced the use of military force without the consent of Congress, citing as examples the invasion of Grenada and the first Gulf War. "The Constitution stipulates that only Congress can declare war," said Stokes.

**"The so-called religious right is a very dangerous group of people. Many of the things they espouse are a real threat to democracy."**

The retired congressman was discouraged about the prospects for health care reform. "You would think," he said, "that a nation that just announced yesterday we anticipate a $1 trillion surplus in the federal budget over the next fifteen years would be able to afford health care for every American." Republicans, Stokes said, defeated President Clinton's comprehensive health care bill, "but they had the help of Democrats."

Stokes expressed doubt about any legislative action on global warming. On the quality of the federal courts with respect to human and civil rights, Stokes said that with the appointment of some extremely conservative justices to the Supreme Court "we've seen the erosion of gains." Asked whether human rights and international trade ought to be linked, the retired congressman answered affirmatively, pointing out that "the Jackson-Vanik Amendment is still the law."[4]

When asked his opinion of the Clinton presidency, Stokes didn't hesitate: "Had it not been for the Monica Lewinsky affair, President Clinton would have gone down in history as one of the greatest presidents this country has ever seen." He ticked off his accomplishments—the $1 trillion surplus ("something not seen since 1951"), a soaring stock market, low unemployment, our heightened international stature—adding, "On intellect alone, he is one of the most brilliant men in the world."

Will he support Vice President Al Gore in his bid to succeed President Clinton? Stokes demurred, muttered something about "keeping his options open," and laughed heartily as he stepped away from the podium amid warm applause.

4. The Jackson-Vanik Amendment (Section 401, Title IV of the Trade Act of 1974, P.L. 93-618) affected U.S. trade relations with communist or former communist countries that restricted freedom of emigration and other human rights. It was repealed in 2012.

JANUARY 15      AUGUST 6      SEPTEMBER 17

### Dr. Nancy W. Dickey

The president of the American Medical Association, Dr. Nancy W. Dickey, said changes must be made in the health care insurance system. "Every time someone goes to the doctor's office, or your employer pays your insurance, you are helping in the cost to pay for the uninsured 44 million," she said. "It would be far more inexpensive to find a mechanism to give them access to an insurance plan."

### Geoffrey Mearns

Geoffrey Mearns, who spent months working with the U.S. attorney general's office to convict Terry Nichols in connection with the Oklahoma City bombing, recalled some of the people whose lives changed forever when the Alfred P. Murrah Federal Building was blown up on the morning of April 19, 1995, killing 168 people. One woman who survived attended the funerals of 20 friends in 10 days. Another dropped off her one-year-old son at day care and never saw him again. Nichols was convicted of conspiring with former Army buddy Timothy McVeigh in the bombing and was sentenced to life in prison. McVeigh was sentenced to death.[5]

### Julian Bond

"Jim Crow may be dead, but racism is alive and well," NAACP Chairman Julian Bond told the City Club. Bond recalled the organization's history of fighting segregation and racism since its inception in 1909. These days, he said, the civil rights organization struggles against school vouchers (which he called "public welfare for private schools"), the abolition of affirmative-action programs, and House and Senate leaders who are "hostile" to civil rights.

5. Timothy McVeigh was executed in 2001.

JOHN KUNTZ/THE PLAIN DEALER/LANDOV

SEPTEMBER 23

### Archbishop Desmond Tutu

In an appearance jointly sponsored with the City of Cleveland as part of a series to mark the approaching millennium, Archbishop Desmond Tutu preached a message of racial unity from the podium in Cleveland Music Hall. A towering leader in the dismantling of apartheid in South Africa, Tutu suggested that Cleveland might be a model for the world of a new kind of compassionate society. "You in this city have an opportunity . . . to be an audio and visual aid for people to see what God intends us to be. They look at Cleveland, with seventy-seven different ethnic groups, who celebrate who they are, who rejoice in their diversity."

**Will Rogers**, president of the Trust for Public Land

**Steven Brill**, journalist and founder of *Court TV* and *American Lawyer* magazine

**Rev. Joan Brown Campbell**, general secretary, National Council of Churches

**Helen Thomas**, trailblazing White House correspondent in a press corps dominated by men

**Robert M. Morgenthau**, district attorney for New York County, the borough of Manhattan

## David S. Broder
May 12, 2000

David Broder's fourth appearance at the City Club coincided with the club's return to its newly renovated quarters, and as he took the podium the senior political columnist for the *Washington Post* admired the "transformation that has been wrought here." Then, alluding to the traditional question-and-answer period, he observed that "the fun and games begin when the speaker shuts up" and promised to be brief.

Broder opened his talk with some general comments about the current presidential election campaign pitting George W. Bush, the Republican governor of Texas, against Senator Al Gore, Democrat from Tennessee. "We're looking at an extraordinary, high-stakes election," he said, that will determine the presidency and could alter the tenor of Congress and, over time, the makeup of the Supreme Court. "In six months, we will decide who writes the laws and who interprets the laws," and in Congress "the shift of six seats" would change the makeup of the committee chairs. As an example, he cited the powerful House Ways and Means Committee, chaired by Bill Archer, who, he said, represents a silk-stocking district in Houston, Texas. Depending on which way the elections go, it could be led instead by Charles Rangel, who represents Harlem.

But the astute political analyst wanted to talk about "another side to this election": the ever more prevalent and popular ballot initiative. "Increasingly," he said, "the most fundamental decisions are made by ballot and not legislators."

The ballot initiative was brought to the United States about a century ago by populists and progressives from Switzerland as a means of empowering people shut out of power by legislators "bought and paid for" by corporate interests. About half the states, he said, allow initiatives, in which petitions are circulated for the purpose of placing an issue on the ballot. Broder gave some examples, noting that animal rights advocates had been particularly successful using the process. But, he observed, the ballot initiative is "now being highjacked by special interests." He gave the example of George Soros, the business magnate and philanthropist, who "believes that the war on drugs is dumb" and has financed ballot initiatives to legalize drugs in six states.

Broder paused for a quick history lesson, reminding the audience that the Founding Fathers wanted a strong but limited government and believed that the majority vote can be "unstable." They gave us, not a democracy, but a republic, with checks and balances to protect minority views and prevent what he called "the sentiment of the moment" from holding sway. Two houses of Congress, together with the committee structure in both, allow for discussion and compromise among competing interests to achieve consensus—something that ballot initiatives do not do. Broder said he was "not so sure" that ballot initiatives, an increasingly powerful and popular form of lawmaking, were a good idea.

In response to a question from the audience, the columnist acknowledged that "there are advantages and there are risks" with initiatives, expressing concern that they are often used "not as a last resort but as the first choice, as a way of shortcutting representative government." Further, anyone with enough money can buy one. The wealthy, someone told him at the Commonwealth Club in Silicon Valley, have "gone from having trophy wives to trophy initiatives."

**"Increasingly, the most fundamental decisions are made by ballot and not legislators."**

Asked to speculate on the outcome of the fall election, Broder said, tongue-in-cheek, "I actually know the answer, but my contract with the *Washington Post* says it's got to appear there first." He did predict that it would be close.

Asked who, if he were a senior advisor to Bush and Gore, he would propose as each man's vice-presidential candidate, Broder said, "I'm permanently barred from speculating about the vice-presidential choice, both inside and outside the newsroom. The last time I was right—the only time I was right—the name was Spiro Agnew." The room erupted in laughter.

MAY 5

MAY 19

JULY 14

### Rep. John Lewis

Speaking to a Law Day luncheon organized by two area bar associations and the City Club, Representative John Lewis, a Democrat from Georgia, recalled his experiences as a student activist during the civil rights movement in the 1960s, when, he said, many lawyers and judges played a key role in ending segregation by protecting people who organized sit-ins and marches in the South. "I came here to say to you, as members of the bar and bench, thank you . . . for using the law as a tool to help build a truly integrated society."

### Gregory B. Craig

Gregory B. Craig, a lawyer who defended President Clinton during his impeachment and who was then representing Juan Miguel González in his bid to return with his six-year-old son Elián to Cuba, had to fax his speech to the City Club when his flight was canceled because of inclement weather. Craig's prepared remarks (which were read by City Club member Rick Taft) focused solely on the impeachment. "I am still appalled," he said, "at how close the government of the United States came to unraveling—legally, constitutionally, politically, morally." All of the questions that followed were about the González case. Craig said, by telephone, that there was "an arrogance" in America that does not understand why anyone would not want to live here, adding that González is a simple and apolitical man who wants to go home with his son.

### Louis Caldera

Army Secretary Louis Caldera said the U.S. Army is retooling to have the capability to fight cyber-wars against military governments controlled by drug cartels. Such partnerships are emerging as likely security risks to the United States. He did not give any examples but called overseas drug cartels "intelligent and adaptive adversaries who are looking at the advantages that technology and weapons of mass destruction give them."

DECEMBER 8

**Pat Robertson**
In wide-ranging remarks, religious leader Pat Robertson, founder and chairman of the Christian Broadcasting Network, called on Vice President Al Gore to concede the Florida presidential election results ("I kind of think he's making a fool of himself") and credited President Bill Clinton for the thriving economy ("All his escapades notwithstanding, we've got money in our pockets"). Robertson also applauded Clinton for proposing that the United States forgive the debt of impoverished nations. Freeing poor countries to dedicate more funding to reduce hunger and improve housing and employment, he said, is consistent with Christian principles.

**Sarah Bloomfield**, executive director, United States Holocaust Memorial Museum

**Martin McGuinness**, chief negotiator for Sinn Fein

**Roy Bourgeois**, a laicized Roman Catholic priest and founder of the human rights group School of the Americas Watch

**Robert Putnam**, Peter and Isabel Malkin Professor of Public Policy, Harvard University, and author of *Bowling Alone: The Collapse and Revival of American Community*

**Tom Brazaitis** and **Eleanor Clift**, husband-and-wife journalists and co-authors of *Madam President: Women Blazing the Leadership Trail*

## William A. McDonough
April 20, 2001

The key to saving the planet isn't more regulations but better design, according to William McDonough. "I see design as the first signal of human intention," declared the Tokyo-born, Yale-trained architect and principal of William McDonough + Partners in Charlottesville, Virginia. He posed two questions: "How do we love all children of all species for all time? And, when did we become natives of this place?"

"We can look out at our planet and see tragedies in the making," he said—air and water pollution, global warming, toxic chemicals, nuclear waste. "We can't say we didn't intend for these things to happen. It's our de facto plan."

For five years McDonough lived in a house designed by Thomas Jefferson—Monticello—and absorbed its lessons. Jefferson's tombstone, McDonough said, records "only his designs": author of the Declaration of Independence and the Virginia Statute for Religious Freedom, and father of the University of Virginia. "What was this 33-year-old revolutionary thinking when he wrote the Declaration of Independence?" McDonough asked. He was thinking about life, liberty, and the pursuit of happiness, and freedom from remote tyranny. He never contemplated the right to pollute.

Ralph Waldo Emerson considered nature to be "all those things too big for humans to affect"—the oceans, for example. Even in his own time, however, his definition did not hold up. The transcendentalist traveled to Europe on a sailing ship powered by wind; he returned on a steamship powered by coal fed into boilers, spewing smoke and ash into the air.

> **"We gave people daylight [and] fresh air; they listen to the Beach Boys, wear sunglasses, make furniture, and productivity is up 24 percent. Go figure."**

McDonough challenged the audience to think about the Industrial Revolution as a design assignment. "You're designers," he said. "Let me ask you this: Could you design a system . . . [that would] put billions of pounds of highly hazardous materials into your water, air, and soil every year; measure your prosperity by how much natural 'capital' you can dig up, cut down, bury, burn, or otherwise destroy; measure productivity by how few people are working; measure progress by your number of smokestacks; require thousands of complex regulations to keep you from killing each other too quickly; destroy biological and cultural diversity at every turn, seeking one-size-fits-all solutions all over the world, and, while you're at it, leave a few things behind that are so highly toxic that they'll require thousands of generations to live with complex maintenance while living in terror? Could you do that?"

In McDonough's view, that is the legacy of the Industrial Revolution. But "eco-efficiency—doing more with less—is not going to save us. It's merely *less bad*." Nor is McDonough interested in sustainability. "There's no excitement there," he said dismissively. "The real question is: Are you doing the right thing? If you follow nature's laws, growth can be good," said McDonough.

With his partner, the chemist Michael Braungart, McDonough coined the term *eco-effectiveness* to describe his firm's approach. It champions changing our ecological footprint from asphalt to wetlands, adopting porous paving, closed-loop manufacturing, fabrics "safe enough to eat" (made in a mill whose effluent is clean enough to drink), and "infinitely recyclable" polyester and nylon.

For Ford Motor Company in Dearborn, Michigan, McDonough designed a truck-assembly plant with a 450,000-square-foot habitat on the roof. "Ford," he said, "has declared itself native to Dearborn," adding, "GM never declared itself native to Flint."

For Herman Miller, McDonough designed an award-winning furniture factory in Zeeland, Michigan. "We gave people daylight [and] fresh air; they listen to the Beach Boys, wear sunglasses, make furniture, and productivity is up 24 percent. Go figure."

For Gap, he designed a new corporate campus with "an undulating meadow of the ancient grasses of San Bruno" on the roof. "The birds look down and recognize their habitat . . . The people say things like 'Thank God it's Monday.'"

"Wouldn't it be marvelous," the architect summed up, "if that thing that human beings have that identifies us as a separate species, that honors our creativity, our intuition, our intentionality, and our hope—if we could design things that would allow all of our children's children's children's children's children's children's children to celebrate life, liberty, and the pursuit of happiness, free from the intergenerational remote tyranny that is us."

MARCH 16　　　　OCTOBER 17　　　　OCTOBER 19

### Rosabeth Moss Kanter

Nobody knows how the Internet ultimately will reshape the economy or change the way we live and work, but every organization will be affected, said Rosabeth Moss Kanter, a Harvard Business School professor and an expert in organizational change. She appeared at the City Club to promote her book, *Evolve! Succeeding in the Digital Culture of Tomorrow.* Human relationships encourage creativity and collaboration in the workplace, she said, and the best Internet-related companies still rely on face-to-face meetings.

### Larry Kellner
### Jeff Smisek

Little more than a month following the September 11 terrorist attacks, Continental Airlines President Larry Kellner reported that the company's financial situation was improving as more travelers return to the skies. The airline is now losing $6 million a day, compared with $10 million a day in late September, but tightened security has resulted in backups. "It's a facilities issue that we need to fix," said Continental Executive Vice President Jeff Smisek.

### Michael Milken

An overflow crowd heard Michael Milken address what he sees as the nation's economic challenges: public access to capital, knowledge, and health care. The junk bond king and felon-turned-philanthropist (Milken pleaded guilty to securities fraud and other charges in 1990 and served twenty-two months in federal prison) cited, among the nation's financial strides in the last three decades, less reliance on traditional banks. Mortgages held by second or third parties, he said, have made it difficult to discriminate by age, race, or religion.

NOVEMBER 16

**Dr. David Satcher**
U.S. Surgeon General David Satcher said the country treats mental illness effectively but does a poor job of preventing it. "One-fifth of Americans—44 million adults and 14 million children—experience a mental disorder each year," he said. Satcher's remarks to the capacity crowd also touched on bioterrorism, the September 11 attacks, and the war in Afghanistan.

**Ted Gup**, Shirley Wormser Professor of Journalism, Case Western Reserve University, and author of *The Book of Honor: Covert Lives and Classified Deaths*

**Michael Porter**, professor, Harvard Business School, a leading authority on industrial clusters and the competitiveness of nations and regions

**F. X. Toole**, the pen name of boxing trainer Jerry Boyd, author of a collection of short stories titled *Rope Burns: Stories from the Corner*, which were adapted into the Oscar-winning movie *Million Dollar Baby* (2004)

**Deborah Tannen**, professor of linguistics, Georgetown University, and author of *You Just Don't Understand: Women and Men in Conversation*

**Lee C. Bollinger**, president of the University of Michigan

# 2002

## Hassan Abdel Rahman
May 10, 2002

> "How can you offer other people a land that is [already] inhabited?"

The chief representative of the Palestine Liberation Organization (PLO) in the United States passionately dissected the Israeli-Palestinian conflict, calling it "one of the most written-about conflicts in the world and one of the least understood." Hassan Abdel Rahman spoke to a large and visibly divided audience in the ballroom of the Sheraton City Centre Hotel. Security was tight; each person entering the room had to pass through a metal detector.

As an active participant in the peace process since 1974, when the U.N. granted the PLO observer status, Abdel Rahman said, "I have always advocated a two-state solution: a Palestinian state in the West Bank and Gaza, using the 1967 boundaries, living in peace with Israel. Twenty-seven years later, my dream has not been realized. Today the Palestinians still live either under illegal foreign occupation or in exile as refugees."

Abdel Rahman said that, in the United States, the Palestinian side of the story has not been told. He used his speech to deliver "a Palestinian perspective on the past and our hopes for the future."

The nature of the conflict is not "Muslims versus Jews," he said. "Arabs too are Semites, and Arabs and Jews are both the children of Abraham. No, this is a conflict between Zionism and Palestinian nationalism—a conflict that began with Jewish immigration to Palestine following the Balfour Declaration of 1917."

"The Jews did not come to live as do immigrants to other lands, as citizens of Palestine," he said. "They came with one idea: to create a Jewish state." Until the First World War, Palestine for centuries had been part of the Ottoman Empire, but it enjoyed autonomy—with its own heritage and its own customs, said Abdel Rahman. After the First World War, Great

Britain, which controlled Palestine, became allied with Zionists in Europe. The Balfour Declaration promised a homeland for the Jews, at the same time promising to protect the civil and religious rights of existing non-Jewish communities in Palestine.

"How," asked Abdel Rahman, "can you offer other people a land that is [already] inhabited?" Jewish immigrants who arrived under the British Mandate, he said, created their own colonies and did not mix with the existing population. Then, with the creation of Israel by the United Nations in 1948, "Palestine ceased to exist. We became a state-less people."

This history underscored Abdel Rahman's central point: "*Denial* does not help the confidence that we need to build [peace] with and among each other. We have to acknowledge the injustice in order to be able to correct it and overcome it. American Jewish communities that help to perpetuate this denial of responsibility—[and maintain] that Israel existed always—do not help this effort." Here Abdel Rahman earned strong applause from some audience members; others sat stone-faced, arms folded.

He went on forcefully: "I condemn anyone who denies the Holocaust existed. This is part of the Jewish experience. *It existed*. We the Palestinians have to sympathize with the victims of the Holocaust. But that does not justify for the children of the survivors of the Holocaust to inflict pain on the Palestinians." Some audience members began applauding, but the diplomat quickly silenced them and went on.

"We who were victims came back and said, 'We want to make peace,'" said Abdel Rahman. Despite violence perpetrated by extremists on both sides, "negotiations continued—until [Benjamin] Netanyahu took over [as foreign affairs minister of Israel]." [Prime Minister Ariel] Sharon "went on television and called for more new settlements." New Jewish settlers, mostly from Brooklyn, he charged, harass the Palestinians, and Palestinians daily endure humiliation by the Israeli Army—as they pass through checkpoints, as they collect olives from their own olive trees.

**"We the Palestinians have to sympathize with the victims of the Holocaust. But that does not justify for the children of the survivors of the Holocaust to inflict pain on the Palestinians."**

Israel, said Abdel Rahman, has occupied the West Bank for thirty-six years, during which time it has destroyed the Palestinian infrastructure. "The issue is, how to get out of this quagmire we are in," he said. Abdel Rahman said he was "encouraged" by the peace efforts of President George W. Bush, and he referred to a recent speech by Secretary of State Colin Powell in which Powell said that Israel must end its occupation of the Palestinian territories.

"No nation under military occupation will remain silent," Abdel Rahman concluded. "Peace is possible. The principles, the foundation is there. This is the only option that we have. Because the other option is"—he paused briefly—"God forbid."

In the question-and-answer period (by which time many listeners had walked out), the speaker and audience members traded charges and counter-charges—that Palestinian children are brainwashed to hate Jews, that Israel denies the right to a Palestinian state. The forum closed with the speaker's final words: "Let's not point fingers. Let's look for a way out of this."

MARCH 22                    OCTOBER 3

### Leonard Downie Jr.

Leonard Downie Jr., executive editor of the *Washington Post*, said the Bush administration, in its efforts to control the flow of information in the aftermath of the September 11 attacks, has aided those who want to keep public matters private. "We see more and more efforts to close records. It's a result of terrorism and people's fears," he said, but it is being too broadly applied.

### Richard Florida

Cities seeking economic rejuvenation should lure some of the 38 million workers in the nation's swelling collarless creative class, said urban theorist Richard Florida, author of *The Rise of the Creative Class*. Forget about new convention centers or even tax incentives—think about creating a climate good for people, not just good for business. Creative workers want to live in diverse, quirky neighborhoods, not amid anonymous sprawl, and it's more critical than ever for cities to shape themselves in ways to attract those workers.

DECEMBER 6

## Dr. Jim Yong Kim

Dr. Jim Yong Kim, a Harvard-based physician and anthropologist and the author of *Dying for Growth: Global Inequality and the Health of the Poor*, said the United States should direct more aid to developing countries. AIDS has caused the life expectancy in some countries to drop by more than half, and in five years AIDS in Africa will start having an impact on the global economy.

**Cardinal Theodore McCarrick**, archbishop of Washington

**Jeanette Grasselli-Brown**, a member of the Ohio Board of Regents and a pioneering woman scientist who worked her way from chemist to director of corporate research for BP America

**Franz Welser-Möst**, music director of the Cleveland Orchestra

**Vernon Jordan**, African American lawyer, business executive, and civil rights activist

economist **Alice Rivlin**, who served as the first director of the Congressional Budget Office

### John Glenn
August 29, 2003

Former Senator John Glenn, the first American to orbit the Earth, appeared at the City Club to mark the 100th anniversary of powered flight. Glenn was warmly received by the packed house, in which there was a palpable sense that one was in the presence of a genuine, even beloved American hero.

As a combat aviator in the Marine Corps, Glenn served his country in both World War II and the Korean War. He was one of the Mercury Seven, the elite U.S. military test pilots selected by the National Aeronautics and Space Administration (NASA) to operate the experimental Mercury spacecraft and become the first American astronauts. On February 20, 1962, piloting the *Friendship 7*, he became the first American to orbit the Earth. Then, on October 29, 1998, at age 77, Glenn returned to space, lifting off on space shuttle *Discovery* to study the effects of space flight on the elderly.

**"From the sand of Kitty Hawk to the dust of the moon was only 66 years."**

If man was meant to fly, God would have given us feathers, the naysayers loved to point out, Glenn said. That was before two Dayton, Ohio, bicycle makers succeeded in reaching an altitude of 852 feet and remained airborne for 59 seconds at Kitty Hawk, North Carolina, on December 17, 1903.

Back home, brothers Orville and Wilbur Wright—"methodical men with tenacity," Glenn called them—doggedly continued their experiments as they sought to master the *control* of flight, inventing truly maneuverable flight at Huffman Prairie outside of Dayton.

World War I provided an important impetus to airplane development. In the United States, the Army's Signal Corps put out the first government specifications, which, Glenn noted with amusement, were contained on a single page and called for an airplane capable of reaching "at least 40 miles per hour."

Orville's speed at Kitty Hawk was just 31 m.p.h. "Ever since," said Glenn, "it's been higher faster, higher faster, higher faster." He ticked off the milestones: Forty-four years after Kitty Hawk, Chuck Yeager became the first pilot to travel faster than sound. Fifty-eight years later Alan Shepard became the first man in space. And today's International Space Station travels at 4.86 *miles per second*. Underscoring the breathtaking pace of development, Glenn noted, "From the sand of Kitty Hawk to the dust of the moon was only 66 years."

Glenn, who was born in Cambridge, Ohio, and raised in New Concord, Ohio, recalled his father bringing him to the National Air Races in Cleveland, which drew the best flyers of the time. That experience sowed the seeds of his lifelong interest in aviation. There is still a tremendous amount to learn, said Glenn. "I know of no more humbling experience for any pilot than to observe hummingbirds in flight. We are amateurs by comparison."

A Wright descendant recently presented Glenn with a fragment of cloth from the wing of the plane the brothers flew at Kitty Hawk. "That stained bit of cloth means a lot to me," Glenn said, "for it symbolizes the distance we've come in the last hundred years, and how the opportunities and experiences in my own life were made possible by what the Wright brothers did in Dayton and Kitty Hawk eighteen years before I was born. Growing up, I read about those earlier Ohio boys, but only in my wildest dreams could I have looked forward to flying faster, farther, and higher."

"Curiosity," Glenn said, "is at the heart of all progress. Someone has to think about how we can do things differently, or believe there just may be a better way. But *progress* comes when we not only think about it but we act on that wonder. That's what the Wright brothers did, and they changed the world for all time."

JANUARY 24

JANUARY 24

JUNE 20

### Senator Tom Daschle

At a special City Club breakfast forum, Senate Democratic Leader Tom Daschle unveiled a plan to "jump-start the economy," calling for an immediate tax cut, billions in aid to state and local governments, and an extension of unemployment benefits. "We need an economic plan with a single overriding goal of helping the economy," Daschle said of his proposal, an alternative to recommendations President George W. Bush was expected make in his forthcoming State of the Union Address.

### Antwone Fisher

Antwone Fisher, the author of *Finding Fish* and the screenwriter for the movie *Antwone Fisher* starring Denzel Washington, spoke to a sold-out City Club Forum. The book and movie tell the story of a neglected and abused foster child, in which Fisher recalls his beloved fifth-grade teacher, Brenda Profit—"the woman closest to a mother that I would ever know"—at Parkwood Elementary School in Cleveland and a city boy's excitement at seeing horses and the natural wonders of country life during a week at Hiram House Camp in suburban Moreland Hills.

### Tom Ridge

Homeland Security Director Tom Ridge said that America is "more secure and better prepared than ever." The former Pennsylvania governor said his fledgling agency has beefed up border patrols, emergency-response training, and intelligence gathering. He pointed to surveillance at ports around the world and the improved technology that speeds inspection of cargo, saying "We need to push our security border outward so that our shores are the last, not the first, line of defense."

NOVEMBER 7            DECEMBER 15

### Peter B. Lewis

Insurance mogul and philanthropist Peter B. Lewis announced that he was ending his two-year moratorium on giving to local causes. "It did whatever good it did and it's over," said Lewis, chairman of Progressive Corporation, who received vigorous applause from the capacity crowd. Lewis's disappointment with Case Western Reserve University, to which he had donated $36 million toward the Frank Gehry-designed business school named for Lewis, triggered the ban. Lewis said he is still disappointed with Cleveland in general, but pleased with changes made at the university. The iconoclastic Lewis said he invests in creative people who are honest, open, and willing to collaborate and face challenges.

### Prince Bandar bin Sultan

Saudi Arabia's ambassador to the United States, Prince Bandar bin Sultan, said that Saudi Arabia remained committed to weeding out religious extremists and accused terrorists of perverting Islam for their own purposes. "9/11 was an evil work done to destroy the image and the truth of a great religion," he told the City Club. The envoy defended his country's government, rejecting much of the criticism aimed at the ruling royal family after the September 11 attacks, in which fifteen of the nineteen hijackers were Saudi nationals.

**Tracy Kidder**, Pulitzer Prize-winning writer and author of *Mountains Beyond Mountains: The Quest of Dr. Paul Farmer, a Man Who Would Cure the World*

**Antonin Scalia**, associate justice of the United States Supreme Court

**Amory Lovins**, co-founder and CEO, Rocky Mountain Institute, a nonprofit organization dedicated to sustainability, with a special focus on profitable innovations for energy and resource efficiency

# 2004

## Condoleezza Rice
October 15, 2004

Just eighteen days before the presidential election, National Security Advisor Condoleezza Rice addressed a City Club audience of 900 at a conference center in suburban Westlake, Ohio, where she defended the Bush administration's response to the terrorist attacks of 9/11 and its invasion of Iraq.

Rice began with a progress report: Osama bin Laden is on the run. Three-quarters of Al Qaeda's known leaders and associates have been detained or killed, and we have frozen millions of dollars of Al Qaeda assets. In Afghanistan, dozens of training camps that graduated thousands of trained killers have been destroyed, and the Taliban regime has been overthrown and replaced with a free Afghan government. We have broken up terrorist cells from Europe to Southeast Asia. Pakistan, which formerly recognized the Taliban regime, is now a friend and ally who helped capture Khalid Sheik Mohammad, the operational planner of 9/11, and Pakistani forces are working hard to round up terrorists along the Pakistan-Afghanistan border. Saudi Arabia is shutting down the facilitators and supporters of terrorism. "The results are plain," Rice said. "The terrorists' world is getting smaller . . . and we will not rest until there is no safe place for them to hide."

"A second front in the war on terror," Rice said, "is to stop the spread of the world's deadliest weapons, and the president has made concrete progress in doing so." The president's policy on weapons of mass destruction is "very clear," she said. "Regimes can pursue WMD at great peril and great expense, or [they] can give up their WMD and embark on a path toward better relations with the international community."

> **"The terrorists' world is getting smaller . . . and we will not rest until there is no safe place for them to hide."**

But to achieve "permanent victory" we must do more, Rice said. "We must affirm the truth that when freedom is on the march, America is more secure, and when freedom is in retreat, America is vulnerable." That is why President Bush has broken with sixty years of excusing and accommodating repressive regimes in the Middle East—a policy that hoped to purchase stability at the price of liberty. "The stakes in the Middle East could not be higher," Rice said. "As long as the broader Middle East remains a region of tyranny and despair and anger, it will produce men and movements that threaten the safety of America and our friends."

America's commitment to freedom is helping to spur "a great debate" from Morocco to Jordan to Qatar. "We are seeing elections and new protections for women and the beginnings of political pluralism," Rice said. "In Afghanistan last week, we witnessed extraordinary testimony to the power of the vote." U.S. soldiers reported Afghans lining up hours before sunrise in the fallen snow, waiting to vote. And, "when Iraqis go to the polls next year to elect a government and put behind them their brutal history, democracy's power will be affirmed again."

Rice proceeded to mount a forceful defense of President Bush's decision to invade Iraq. Saddam Hussein, she said, was the only tyrant of our time not only to possess WMD but to use them in acts of mass murder. He manufactured biological and chemical weapons and then refused to account for them. He deceived the United Nations weapons inspectors and was "in material breach" of U.N. Security Council Resolution 1441, which gave him one last chance to disarm. He was waiting for sanctions to end so that he could restart his weapons programs without hindrance, Rice charged, and he was evading the sanctions by cheating the U.N.'s Oil-for-Food program. "The only way to put an end to his ambitions," Rice said, "was to change the regime."

> **"When Iraqis go to the polls next year to elect a government and put behind them their brutal history, democracy's power will be affirmed again."**

"Saddam's brutal outlaw regime was a unique threat to America, to the Middle East, and to the world," Rice said. "The threat . . . had been festering for a dozen years with no solution in sight, and after September 11 it was a threat that appeared in a fundamentally different light, because the threat that an outlaw state might pass a weapon of mass destruction to a terrorist state is the greatest danger of our time." As long as Saddam remained in power "he remained the key enemy of hope and progress in the broader Middle East."

Rice acknowledged that the period since the liberation of Iraq has been "difficult." But she said that progress had been made toward establishing "a decent government" that protects the rights of its citizens and allows them to fulfill their aspirations. "The hard work of replacing tyranny with liberty is under way. It is turbulent. All historical changes of this magnitude are," she said. But it is preferable, she contended, to the "false stability" that characterized the world in the days before the twin towers fell.

The war on terror is not a limited engagement, said Rice. This is "the struggle of our time." She likened it to a previous era, when America stood fast against the Soviet threat during the Cold War. Fighting communism was the struggle of that time, she said, and Europe and Asia are safer as a result. "So shall it be in the Middle East," Rice concluded.

SEPTEMBER 8

OCTOBER 7

OCTOBER 14

### Henry Kissinger

Addressing the City Club at the Marriott Hotel Downtown, Henry Kissinger, the former secretary of state and winner of the Nobel Peace Prize, argued for preemptive strikes against terrorists. Kissinger said that security threats to the United States have been "privatized" and no longer come only from other countries. U.S. diplomacy does not work against an enemy who moves everywhere, whose leaders are unknown, and who has no territory to defend.

### Richard Holbrooke

Stumping for Senator John Kerry, Richard Holbrooke, U.S. ambassador to the United Nations in the Clinton administration, said the intelligence failure for pre-war Iraq ranks with that of Pearl Harbor and September 11. "The debate is over," he said, on WMD in Iraq. "If the inspectors were allowed to finish the job, as John Kerry had argued they should, what would they have found?"

### Madeleine Albright

Madeleine Albright, former secretary of state and ambassador to the United Nations under President Bill Clinton, called North Korea "the most dangerous place in the world" because of nuclear weapons there and said President Bush was wrong to go to war against Saddam Hussein before finishing the battle with Osama bin Laden. "The war against Saddam was a choice, not a necessity," said Albright. "Now peace there is a necessity, not a choice."

OCTOBER 22

OCTOBER 25

DECEMBER 3

### Joseph Wilson IV

Former ambassador Joseph Wilson IV argued that the United States is less safe following its invasion of Iraq and that the Bush administration betrayed the nation and the world with misleading statements about mushroom clouds. The career diplomat discussed his assignment from the CIA, in advance of the 2003 invasion, to investigate allegations that Saddam Hussein was attempting to purchase uranium from Niger. Wilson found no such evidence and reported that he believed the claims were false, yet President Bush contradicted Wilson's findings during his 2003 State of the Union Address. After Wilson went public with an op-ed in the *New York Times,* the White House retaliated by revealing to a reporter that Wilson's wife, Valerie Plame, was a CIA agent. Wilson said that the revelation scared his family, but its underlying message also should scare the nation. "Be afraid," he said. "Be very afraid."

### George Soros

"The war on terror was just an excuse for the invasion of Iraq," George Soros told the City Club. The Hungarian-born business magnate and philanthropist has spent more than $25 million in his effort to defeat President George Bush. "The fact that the terrorists are evil doesn't make every action we take good," Soros said. "America has lost credibility as the champion of democracy."

### Leo Gerard

The president of the United Steelworkers International, Leo Gerard, expressed optimism about the U.S. steel industry because of strong Chinese demand. It's a demand that will one day dissipate, though. Gerard said the biggest problem for domestic steelmakers has been U.S. trade policy. President George Bush's decision in 2002 to levy tariffs against foreign steel gave the industry some breathing room, but the tariffs were cut off early after pressure from foreign steel makers and trade officials. "With all due respect, the president talks like John Wayne, but when it came to tariffs he acted like Winnie the Pooh," Gerard said.

**Sandra Pianalto**, president and CEO of the Federal Reserve Bank of Cleveland

**Andy Borowitz**, comedian and author of the satirical column "The Borowitz Report"

**Gina Abercrombie-Winstanley**, diplomat then serving as United States consul general in Jeddah, Saudi Arabia

> "Seventy-five percent of customers who say they are satisfied defect. 'Satisfied' should set off alarm bells."

**Anne Mulcahy**
March 11, 2005

*Forbes* magazine declared the chairman and CEO of Xerox Corporation among the most powerful women in the world, and to watch and listen to her was to understand why. Anne Mulcahy was dynamic and personable, with a ready laugh. Her gaze attached, at some point during her talk, to every pair of eyes in the room. Above all, she was focused on one thing—customer service—and has been since she started working for Xerox as an entry-level sales rep shortly after graduating from college. "I've never stopped selling," she told the City Club, pausing to wonder out loud whether her topic, "The Customer Connection," was august enough for such a hallowed forum.

When Mulcahy took the helm, in 2001, Xerox was on death watch. Revenues were declining. Cash on hand was shrinking. It was $19 billion in debt, and its stock price had plummeted. "I accepted the job with equal parts pride and dread." Pride, because she believed deeply in the company's values and a heritage rooted in the development of the plain paper copier. Dread, because bankruptcy rumors were the daily grist of the business press. Warren Buffet told her, "You weren't promoted—you were drafted into a war you didn't start. You better focus on your customers and lead your people as though their lives depend on your success."

"Nothing focuses the mind like the sight of the gallows," said Mulcahy. She assessed her assets—a loyal customer base that loved the Xerox brand and a committed workforce—and went to work. "Customers told us that we had great technology, employees, and industry experts, but our responsiveness had slipped badly," she said. "Employees told us they'd do whatever it took, but we'd better supply clear and explicit directions about where this company was headed."

Under Mulcahy, Xerox drastically reduced its cost base, doubled its equity, reduced its debt by half, outsourced manufacturing, and increased market capitalization. "In 2000, we lost $273 million," she said, "and in 2004 we made $859 million. Hard work is beginning to yield positive returns."

Having fixed the financial situation and restructured the balance sheet, Mulcahy turned to what she called "the third leg" of the company's turnaround plan: investing in the future of Xerox. "It was important for our people to know that this was going to be a great company again. Even during the darkest days," Mulcahy said, "we didn't take a dollar out of research and development."

Within the half-trillion-dollar annual market for information technology, Xerox moved its focus to color printing, multifunction machines, and lucrative consulting services. Over the past two years, Mulcahy said, "we have introduced seventy-five new products and solutions to the market. Two-thirds of our [current] revenues come from products and services we've introduced in the last two years—a big, important metric for a technology company. Our customers are voting with their checkbooks."

Still, Mulcahy said, "[Employees] were asking what we'd look like when we got through the turnaround. They needed to have a vision of why it was worth staying." So she provided one, writing in 2001 an op-ed for the *Wall Street Journal* describing "the company we wanted to be in 2005."

> **"It was important for our people to know that this was going to be a great company again. Even during the darkest days we didn't take a dollar out of research and development."**

Under Mulcahy, Xerox is on a mission to put the customer first, in keeping with the words of former CEO Joe Wilson: "Customers determine whether we have a job or we do not." She laid out its guiding principles. Among them, listening and innovating with the customer in mind; investing in research and development even in the worst of times; ensuring that everyone is thinking about customer value; and providing great service. On the last point, Mulcahy observed that "75 percent of customers who say they are satisfied defect. 'Satisfied' should set off alarm bells."

Business improvement does not come in a box, Mulcahy said, and productivity is not embedded in software code. "We've got a long way to go," she concluded. "Customers put a lot of trust in us, and we want to deliver a great return on that trust."

JANUARY 21

FEBRUARY 24

MARCH 4

**Dr. Delos "Toby" Cosgrove**

The chief executive of the Cleveland Clinic, Dr. Delos "Toby" Cosgrove, announced that supporting local schools will be the Clinic's No. 1 charitable activity. A portion of its monetary pledge—$10 million over five years—will be used to connect Cleveland high schools to the OneCommunity high-speed broadband network. "If we are to stimulate and help build the economy of Northeast Ohio, we must address the realities of the knowledge economy," Cosgrove said. "We must educate our children and retain and attract the best and the brightest" to Greater Cleveland.

**Senator Bill Frist**

Speaking at the Cleveland Marriott Downtown, Senate Majority Leader Bill Frist said that medical malpractice lawsuits are the top reason for rising medical insurance premiums and the American Medical Association "has designated Ohio right at the top of states in crisis." The threat of lawsuits has forced doctors to practice defensive medicine—"ordering every test I possibly can . . . to defend myself in court." Frist, Republican of Tennessee, is a heart surgeon.

**Imad Moustapha**

Imad Moustapha, Syria's ambassador to the United States, spoke to the City Club amid mounting international pressure to remove its troops and intelligence agents from neighboring Lebanon. Little more than two weeks earlier, Rafic Hariri, the former prime minister of Lebanon, a leader of the anti-Syrian opposition, was killed, along with 21 others, when explosives were detonated as his motorcade drove near the St. George Hotel in Beirut. "Everybody knows that [Syria] went into Lebanon to end a bloody civil war," said the ambassador. "We did not go in there as occupiers or invaders."

AUGUST 19

**Dr. Julie Gerberding**
Dr. Julie Gerberding, head of the Centers for Disease Control and Prevention, told a packed City Club that the nation ought to be able to solve its persistent problem with flu vaccine shortages. "Let's get this issue off the table," she said.

**Connie Schultz**, Pulitzer Prize-winning columnist for the *Cleveland Plain Dealer*

**Rep. Barney Frank**, Democrat of Massachusetts

**Henry Cisneros**, former secretary of housing and urban development under President Bill Clinton and founder and chairman of CityView, whose stated mission is to provide "smart capital for smart growth"

**Robert Barr**, chairman of the board of Liberty Guard, a nonpartisan political education group focused on protecting personal liberty, and a former Republican congressman from Georgia who attained national prominence as a leader of President Bill Clinton's impeachment

## President George W. Bush
March 20, 2006

Three years after launching a preemptive strike against Iraqi President Saddam Hussein and amid growing doubt about the course of the war, President George W. Bush embarked on a speaking tour in an attempt to reassure the American people that the United States was winning the war.

"The central front in the war on terror is Iraq," he told a large City Club audience at the Renaissance Cleveland Hotel, "and in the past few weeks we have seen horrific images coming out of that country." Although Iraq's elected leaders were working to form a unity government, he said, "the situation on the ground remains tense, and in the face of continuing reports about killings and reprisals, I understand how some Americans have had their confidence shaken. Others look at the violence they see each night on their television screens and they wonder how I can remain so optimistic about the prospects of success in Iraq. They wonder what I see that they don't."

Bush then told the story of Tal Afar, a city of 200,000 located about 35 miles from the Syrian border in northern Iraq. Most are Sunni Muslims of Turkmen origin; about a quarter are Shiites. Following the removal of Saddam Hussein, in April 2003, terrorists began moving into Tal Afar, which quickly became a strategic location for Al Qaeda in Iraq and its leader Abu Musab al-Zarqawi. Their objectives, said the president, are to drive us out of Iraq so they can take control, to overthrow moderate Muslim governments throughout the region, and to use Iraq as a base from which to launch attacks against the United States.

In Tal Afar, the terrorists forged "an alliance of convenience" with those who benefited from Saddam's reign and others with their own grievances. They exploited a weak economy to recruit young men to their cause, and within eighteen months they had "basically seized control" of Tal Afar. Coalition forces succeeded in routing them but then moved on, leaving the job of maintaining order to the local police, who rarely ventured out owing to threats against their family members. Once again Al Qaeda moved in, taking over mosques, schools, even the hospital. Kidnappings, bombings,

**"The decision to remove Saddam Hussein was a difficult decision; the decision to remove Saddam Hussein was the right decision."**

and beheadings multiplied in a deliberate attempt to maintain control through intimidation of the populace. The terrorists preyed on adolescents, said the president, who told the story of one Iraqi teenager taken from his family and offered a chance to "prove his manhood" by holding the legs of captives as they were beheaded. "The result of this barbarity was a city where normal life had virtually ceased . . . This is the brutal reality that Al Qaeda wishes to impose on all the people of Iraq."

"We recognized the problem [at Tal Afar] and we changed our strategy," Bush said. Instead of clearing out the terrorists and moving on, Iraqi and coalition forces adopted a new approach of clear, hold, and build. They trained an effective police force and eliminated safe havens in the surrounding towns. Then, block by block, ten Iraqi battalions and ten coalition battalions secured the city. During two weeks of intense fighting, they killed 150 ter-

rorists and captured 850 others. Iraqi forces, together with coalition troops embedded with them, then moved in to hold the city, offer humanitarian assistance, and rebuild.

Today, said President Bush, the terrorists are gone, the citizens of Tal Afar enjoy security, children are in school, and new construction is under way. "The strategy is working," he said. "The people of Tal Afar have shown why spreading liberty and democracy is at the heart of our strategy to defeat the terrorists."

Elsewhere in Iraq, especially in and around Baghdad, the president admitted, savage violence continues. "But the progress made in bringing more Iraqi security forces on line is helping to bring peace and stability to [other] Iraqi cities. The example of Tal Afar gives me confidence in our strategy because in the city we see the outlines of the Iraq that we and the Iraqi people have been fighting for: a free and secure people who are getting back on their feet, who are participating in government and civic life, and who have become allies in the fight against the terrorists."

He continued, "We're gonna help the Iraqis build a strong democracy that will be an inspiration throughout the Middle East—a democracy that will be a global partner in the war against the terrorists." The president's next line, late in the speech, elicited the first applause: "The decision to remove Saddam Hussein was a difficult decision; the decision to remove Saddam Hussein was the right decision."

"In the war on terror we face a global enemy," he continued, "and if we were not fighting this enemy in Iraq, they would not be idle. They would be plotting and trying to kill Americans across the world and within our own borders. Against this enemy there can be no compromise, so we will fight them in Iraq, we will fight them across the world, and we will stay in the fight until the fight is won. In the long run, the best way to defeat this enemy and to ensure the security of our own citizens is to spread the hope of freedom across the Middle East."

"Freedom will prevail in Iraq. Freedom will prevail in the Middle East," said the president, who warned that more sacrifice and tough fighting lie ahead.

JANUARY 13

MAY 5

JULY 21

### Richard Pound

Richard Pound, chairman of the World Anti-Doping Agency, said performance-enhancing drugs have gone from being a sports problem to a public health issue on a par with the international trade of illegal narcotics—and major professional sports share the blame. The sport of cycling, he said, supports a culture of cheating, and he suggested that up to a third of the National Hockey League's players take some form of performance-enhancing drugs. "The next specter coming down the track is genetic manipulation," predicted Pound.

### Vinton Cerf

Vinton Cerf, one of the fathers of the Internet, addressed the City Club on the eve of his induction into the Inventors Hall of Fame in Akron. In the 1970s Cerf, together with Robert Kahn, designed the protocol that today supports everything from e-mail to eBay. In his talk, Cerf addressed the brewing debate over the future of "network neutrality," the so-called First Amendment of the Internet, which keeps an AT&T or Time Warner from charging website operators access rates and ensures that all of a network provider's subscribers can access the content provider's website.

### Moshe Ya'alon

The former head of the Israel Defense Forces, Moshe Ya'alon, said conflict sparking recent bloodshed in the Middle East is not just Israel's battle but is a challenge facing the entire Western world. He singled out Iran as the chief purveyor of radical jihad and an instigator of border raids resulting in the recent confrontations between Israeli forces and the Palestinian Hamas faction and the Hezbollah in Lebanon. Given the additional possibility of Iran developing nuclear weapons, Ya'alon said, "Iran should be stopped. Without confronting Iran—politically, economically and, if necessary, militarily—there is no chance for stability in the region."

## OCTOBER 27

### DEBATE

**Senator Mike DeWine**
**Rep. Sherrod Brown**

A feisty debate in a closely watched Senate race as Democrats aimed to take control of Congress pitted Republican Senator Mike DeWine against Democratic Representative Sherrod Brown. DeWine said Brown had passed few bills during his seven terms in Congress and accused him of running a "scandal-ridden office" during his tenure as Ohio secretary of state two decades earlier. Brown said DeWine and the Bush administration refused to acknowledge the failures in Iraq and the ballooning deficit, and pointed to the loss of 200,000 manufacturing jobs in Ohio.

**Tex G. Hall**, tribal chairman of Three Affiliated Tribes (the Mandan, Hidatsa, and Arikara peoples), twice elected president of the National Congress of American Indians

**Hanan Ashrawi**, Palestinian legislator, activist, and scholar

**Kevin Phillips**, political commentator and author of *American Theocracy: The Peril and Politics of Radical Religion, Oil, and Borrowed Money in the 21st Century*

**Christine Todd Whitman**, former governor of New Jersey and former administrator of the Environmental Protection Agency, author of *It's My Party, Too: The Battle for the Heart of the GOP and the Future of America*

**Richard Louv**, author of *Last Child in the Woods: Saving Our Children from Nature-Deficit Disorder*

**Douglas Wilder**, mayor of Richmond, Virginia, and former governor of Virginia

## Geoffrey Canada

December 3, 2007

"We have a crisis," Geoffrey Canada declared after warming up the large audience with humorous accounts of his guest appearances on *60 Minutes* and *Oprah*. "We are losing the next generation."

Canada, president and CEO of the Harlem Children's Zone (HCZ) in New York City, was speaking at the Fatima Family Center in Cleveland's Hough neighborhood as part of the City Club in the City series. His presentation was lively and, with its hard truths leavened by humor, not unlike a comedian's monologue.

He told listeners about a recent report by the Children's Defense Fund with the sobering title "The Cradle to Prison Pipeline," which said that 480,000 black males are serving sentences in state and federal prisons, while fewer than 40,000 are earning college degrees.

He held up a news clipping and read the headline: "Law on Young Offenders Causes Rhode Island Furor." In Rhode Island, the article said, it costs $39,000 a year to lock up an adult offender. It costs $98,000 a year to lock up a teenage offender. So, to save money, the state has decided to lower the age for "adults" to seventeen.

"What kind of country does that?" Canada asked, his decibel level rising. The tall, lanky, African American educated at Bowdoin and Harvard had other ideas.

"Why couldn't we intervene in a system like this? We knew those kids were in trouble in the second grade," he says. "The system is broken, and it's happening from one end of America to the other. We lock up more people than any other country in the world. How do we remain a superpower?"

Canada sought to empower the audience. "Even the highest officials in the country don't have a clue," he said. "Presidents, cabinet secretaries ask *me*, 'What do you think we ought to do, Geoff?' *They don't have a clue.* That's why *you* must save our children."

> "We lock up more people than any other country in the world. How do we remain a superpower?"

"We have been playing not to win," Canada said. It is not a resource issue—it is an issue of will. During the Clinton administration, the nation enjoyed a trillion-dollar surplus but never used it. Under George Bush, the trillion-dollar surplus turned into a trillion-dollar deficit.

In Harlem, Canada set out to increase the high school and college graduation rates of the children living in a single block by providing a range of support services and actively following their development beginning at birth. HCZ now serves twenty-four square blocks and has since saved 10,000 children. But he cautioned the audience: "You can't do *one* thing—for example, teenage pregnancy prevention; you've got to do *everything*. The question is, for how many children can you do everything?"

Canada outlined his six-step program:

1. Begin early—"before the baby's even here!" (He was practically shouting.) Teach parents about brain development, about good nutrition, from the moment of conception. Then, teach them to talk to the baby, sing to the baby, read to the baby.

2. Create a continuum of programs that follow the child straight through college. "Two hundred eighty of our children are currently in college. Do you know what that's going to mean for Harlem [someday], to have *one hundred kids* coming home with college degrees each year?"

3. Engage parents as partners. Canada acknowledged the challenge of parents who are working, many barely making it. But we have to try.

4. Schools must be redesigned for success. "The school year doesn't make any sense"—except for middle- and upper-class kids from homes with books and other opportunities for cultural enrichment. Canada described a vicious circle: "Kids are failing? Hire another superintendent. Repeat." It's not just the schools' and the teachers' fault, he said. It's a *system* designed for failure.

5. Communities must be support mechanisms for kids. "In the South Bronx, where I grew up," Canada recalled, "adults were the eyes on the street. Mrs. Lipscomb's 'job' was to watch everything going on from her front window. *I hated Mrs. Lipscomb! I couldn't get away with anything!* Mrs. Lipscomb would immediately call my mother." Adults must be prepared to stand up and say, "We will not accept this behavior from you!"

6. Use teacher evaluation as a tool to improve student performance. "Not everyone is designed to work with these children. We need a system that says, 'You've got to produce or you've got to leave.'"

Canada closed with a trite piece of advice—"We've got to think outside the box"—that he illustrated with an anecdote from his college years.

As a social science major at Bowdoin, Canada struggled with statistics. After earning 37 on a test, he went to his teacher for help. The teacher empathized and said, "Geoff, the reason you're not getting it is because that textbook is written 'on a slant.' Here, try this one." Canada went back to the first book, reread the chapter, tried to work the problems, but still didn't get it. He picked up the second book, the one without the "slant." He read the chapter and worked the problems. "I finally got it!" Only later did he realize that there was no "slant"—in either book. "My teacher had simply figured out a way to get me to work twice as hard!" The audience howled, following which Canada closed with an inspirational poem and received a standing ovation.

FEBRUARY 28     MARCH 26     MARCH 30

### Juan Williams

Journalist Juan Williams, author of *Enough: The Phony Leaders, Dead-End Movements and Culture of Failure that are Undermining Black America*, touched on the controversial topics that underpin his latest book. He excoriated African American leaders who have failed to pass the torch because they're busy guarding their turf. "Stop romanticizing the fifties and sixties and start talking about what's happening right now," he said.

### Elizabeth Edwards

Four days after she and her husband, Senator John Edwards, Democrat of North Carolina, announced that she had Stage 4 breast cancer, Elizabeth Edwards gave a personal account of her ongoing battle with the disease and talked about its meaning for her husband's presidential campaign.

### Billie Jean King

In a program marking the 35th anniversary of Title IX,[6] *USA Today* sports columnist Christine Brennan interviewed tennis great Billie Jean King. King told the City Club that she realized the goal she set for herself at age eleven—to become the No. 1 tennis player in the world—but that she was nowhere near ready to retire. As a founder of the Women Sports Foundation, King promotes the group's nationwide GoGirlGo! initiative to encourage inactive girls aged eight to eighteen to participate in regular physical activity. "Girls don't get the same attention and encouragement [as boys]," she said.

6. Title IX of the Education Amendments of 1972 protects people from discrimination based on sex in education programs and activities that receive federal financial assistance.

JULY 13

**Cecile Richards**
Cecile Richards, president of Planned Parenthood Federation of America and daughter of the late Texas Governor Ann Richards, told the City Club it was important to elect a pro-choice president in 2008. Richards was in Cleveland to announce the consolidation of five independent affiliates to create Planned Parenthood of Northeast Ohio. According to a 2006 study by the Guttmacher Institute, she said, Ohio ranks 48th in state efforts to prevent unwanted pregnancies.

**Kathleen Kennedy Townsend**, former lieutenant governor of Maryland and author of *Failing America's Faithful: How Today's Churches Are Mixing God with Politics and Losing Their Way*

documentary filmmaker **Ken Burns**

economist **Paul Volcker**, former chairman of the Federal Reserve under Presidents Jimmy Carter and Ronald Reagan

**John J. Mearsheimer** and **Stephen M. Walt**, authors of *The Israel Lobby and U.S. Foreign Policy*

*New York Times* technology columnist **David Pogue**

**Donna Shalala**, president of the University of Miami

## Cuyahoga County Treasurer Jim Rokakis
May 28, 2008

By 2008, when Cuyahoga County Treasurer Jim Rokakis addressed the City Club, Cleveland was the epicenter of a national foreclosure crisis. The numbers were staggering. In 1995 there were 3,500 foreclosures in Cuyahoga County. In 2007 there were over 15,000, and 2008 promised—threatened—to match if not exceed that number.

Flippers were buying distressed properties, making nominal repairs, and selling them for three or four times what they paid for them. Mortgage companies, often located out of state, were deceptively convincing borrowers to agree to unfair and abusive loan terms, often targeting the less educated, the poor, and racial minorities, or making loans to fraudulent buyers that they knew would default on the loans. So-called "predatory mortgage lending" had left Cleveland and other communities in Cuyahoga County with a surfeit of vacant and abandoned properties owned by lenders and real-state wholesalers. Vandals were stripping empty houses of everything of value, leaving blighted neighborhoods and exacting a devastating human toll as well.

Rokakis described visiting the county's Board of Revision, where he reviewed the cases of property owners who had filed for a reduction in their real estate taxes. One homeowner, on Ridpath Avenue in the Collinwood neighborhood of Cleveland, reported six vacant houses on his block alone; another, who had lived in her home on Iowa Avenue in the city's Forest Hills area since 1964, wrote on her application, "Foreclosures have ruined this neighborhood, and I have nowhere to go."

> "New Orleans had Hurricane Katrina. We had out-of-control and irresponsible lenders."

Between 2000 and 2008, Cuyahoga County lost 90,000 people, said Rokakis, representing the second-worst population decline in the nation. Only New Orleans lost more. "New Orleans had Hurricane Katrina. We had out-of-control and irresponsible lenders," he said. Rokakis said that in 2008 Cleveland will spend $9 million on demolitions; Shaker Heights will spend a half-million dollars on the maintenance and upkeep of vacant properties. And empty houses and plummeting property values will mean the substantial loss of tax revenue for the schools and general funds of many communities, including, in addition to Cleveland, the inner-ring suburbs of Cleveland Heights, East Cleveland, Euclid, Maple Heights, and Garfield Heights.

"How do we try to restore some semblance of order to this chaotic picture?" Rokakis asked, after painting this bleak picture.

Together with colleagues in county government and others in the city's nonprofit housing agencies (to each of whom he gave generous credit), Rokakis set to work. They studied the pioneering efforts of Dan Kildee, the treasurer of Genesee County, Michigan, where a land bank had taken control of thousands of properties. They crafted legislation—pending before the Ohio Legislature as Rokakis spoke—that will allow Cuyahoga County to create a nonprofit land bank having broad powers, he explained, "to buy, sell,

swap, and hold foreclosed property—to borrow money, receive gifts, and more." The Cuyahoga County Land Bank will have its own income stream from sale of its properties and from penalties and interest on delinquent taxes. Where properties contain structures, those structures will either be rehabilitated or demolished, depending on condition and market potential.

Rokakis stressed that the Cuyahoga County Land Bank is not a quick fix, but rather a "long-term acquire and hold strategy." Results, he cautioned, will come slowly. But he is optimistic that, as the cost of gasoline continues to rise, so will the value of inner-city land. "I have a hard time believing that land close to the Cleveland Clinic, to University Circle, and downtown won't be valuable again," he said.

Rokakis concluded: "If we can use this authority to check, at least in part, the next round of speculators and predators—that will be a good thing. If we can use it as a vehicle to raise money to demolish thousands of vacant properties, arrest the decline in property values, and stabilize neighborhoods—that will be a very good thing. But, if we can say to our kids . . . that we began a process in 2008 that ensured that Northeast Ohio was a better place to raise our children and took back control of our community— that will be a great thing."[7]

7. The real estate flipping game in Cuyahoga County has been stopped. Ohio Senate Bill 373 was passed in December 2008 and Cuyahoga County opened the first land bank in Ohio the following June. By 2013, sixteen other Ohio counties had established land banks, all with the assistance of Jim Rokakis. The Cuyahoga Land Bank has demolished over 2,500 structures and rehabilitated more than 700, and is viewed as a national leader in the effort to create land banks.

JANUARY 18                    FEBRUARY 9

### Zhou Wenzhong

Wrapping up his two-
day visit to Cleveland,
Zhou Wenzhong, China's
ambassador to the United
States, named Cleveland
State University as the home
of a Confucius Institute
during his talk to the City
Club. Aligned with and
financed by the government
of the People's Republic
of China, the institutes
promote Chinese language
and culture, support the
teaching of Chinese, and
facilitate cultural exchanges.

### Ron Gettelfinger

Last year's groundbreaking
labor deals are not enough
to ensure the survival
of America's automotive
industry, said United Auto
Workers President Ron
Gettelfinger. Public policy
also must change to support
manufacturing. The big-
gest thing the government
could do to aid manufac-
turing would be to offer
universal health care, said
Gettelfinger. Most other
auto-producing countries
provide nationalized benefits
instead of depending on
employers to offer coverage.
"How can we compete with
other countries that don't
have the health-care issue?"
he asked.

AUGUST 1

**Gov. Deval Patrick**
As some of the biggest names behind the presidential candidacy of Barack Obama met in Cleveland as part of the Democratic National Committee's three-day platform conference, one of them, Deval Patrick, a close Obama adviser and Massachusetts' first black governor, spoke to the City Club about Democratic priorities.

**Strobe Talbott**,
Washington bureau chief, *Time* magazine

**Dr. Ezekiel Emanuel**,
chief of the Department of Bioethics at the Clinical Center of the National Institutes of Health

**Michael Chertoff**,
secretary of the Department of Homeland Security

**Rajmohan Gandhi**, the grandson of Mahatma Gandhi and author of *Gandhi: The Man, His People, and the Empire*

**Mohsin Hamid**,
author of *The Reluctant Fundamentalist*

## Sister Helen Prejean
September 18, 2009

"Ohio, you have a problem," she began. With a fierce, no-nonsense delivery, Sister Helen Prejean, a member of the Roman Catholic Congregation of St. Joseph, laid out her case against the death penalty.

"One hundred sixty-six people on death row. You've executed thirty-three [since the Supreme Court lifted its moratorium on capital punishment in 1977]." As citizens, she said bluntly, "our hands are in it."

Three days earlier, an execution team in Ohio had tried and failed to find a usable vein in the arm of Romell Broom, convicted of rape and murder in 1984. Lethal injection, Prejean said, is not painless; she vomited the first time she witnessed it. "The closer you get to it, the quicker you reject it."

Prejean, who has witnessed six executions, excoriated Supreme Court Justice Antonin Scalia for having once described lethal injection as "a quiet, enviable death" and for using Romans 13 to justify the death penalty: government, in other words, derives its moral authority from God. Our embrace of capital punishment, Prejean argued, has weakened our morality as a nation.

"We are going through an era in this country where the acceptance of torture has been approved [from] the White House on down, and it provided

**"We are going through an era in this country where the acceptance of torture has been approved [from] the White House on down."**

> **"Do we really think that the way we heal the human wound of having lost a person to violence is to watch as the state kills?"**

the climate" for the abuses at Abu Ghraib and Guantanamo. Like the death penalty, she said, no one sees it: the waterboarding, inmates tied up in stress positions, those (dubbed "frequent fliers") made to move to a different cell every hour as they are subjected to sleep deprivation. "Is this the kind of society we want to be?" she asked.

"When I started out as a nun, I never knew I'd go to death row," she said. Prejean grew up in a well-to-do family in Baton Rouge, Louisiana. She attended all-white private schools; the only African Americans she knew were servants. Her comfortable, private spirituality was shaken when she became the pen pal of Patrick Sonnier, a convicted killer on death row at the Louisiana State Penitentiary. What she saw, Prejean said, led to "an awakening in my own faith about what Jesus was all about" and to her book *Dead Man Walking* (1993).

"We don't think about the death penalty because it doesn't touch our lives. We're afraid of crime, and politicians tell us we've got to get tough on crime . . . The Supreme Court says, 'The death penalty is not for ordinary murderers, only the worst of the worst.' Can anyone tell me what that is?" she asked. "Who has the wisdom to decide? We don't."

Prejean said she once believed that poor defendants going to trial may not have the best attorneys, but at least they would have decent attorneys who would fight for them. But 135 people—wrongly convicted—have come off death row after reexamination of their cases revealed serious mistakes or omissions. Many public defenders receive no more than $12,500 for their services, and although prosecutors are supposed to share their evidence with the defense, volunteers working for the Innocence Project routinely find evidence the jury never heard.

Prejean mentioned the cases of Dobie Gillis Williams and Joseph O'Dell, whose stories she told in her second book, *The Death of Innocents: An Eyewitness Account of Wrongful Executions* (2004). Gillis, an indigent black man with an IQ of 65 whose attorney "did nothing for him," was convicted by an all-white jury. O'Dell, who chose to act as his own attorney, was ambushed late in the trial by a "surprise witness" from the prison, who claimed O'Dell had confessed to the crime. Years later, after O'Dell had been put to death, the witness recanted.

"What about the victims?" Prejean asked. "Do we really think that the way we heal the human wound of having lost a person to violence is to watch as the state kills?" When Timothy McVeigh was executed for the Oklahoma City bombing, in which 168 people were killed, she said, "half the victims' families realized that after watching McVeigh die on closed-circuit television they'd still have to come home and face the empty chair."

In the question-and-answer period, Prejean debunked the contention that the death penalty is a deterrent to crime, saying, "We have a track record now that proves otherwise. We don't need the death penalty to be safe."

| JANUARY 23 | MARCH 30 | APRIL 24 |

### Aaron David Miller

In the aftermath of an Israeli offensive against Hamas in the Gaza Strip that resulted in more than 1,300 Palestinian deaths, as well as 13 Israeli fatalities, Middle East analyst Aaron David Miller said there is "no conflict-ending solution" in sight in Israeli-Palestinian talks, and anyone who attempts such a deal "will fail." Miller, who has served six secretaries of state as an advisor on Arab-Israeli negotiations, instead advocated a new look at an Israeli-Syrian agreement on the Golan Heights.

### John Ging

The director of operations for U.N. humanitarian relief in the Gaza Strip said the only way to end the crisis that created his job will require Israelis and Palestinians to see the humanity in the other side. "No civilians should be at the receiving end of a rocket," said John Ging. Ging said Israel is thwarting Gaza's recovery by restricting the flow of goods and supplies into the territory. "Lifting the siege in Gaza is an urgent, urgent first step" to restoring human dignity.

### Abraham Foxman

Abraham Foxman, the national director of the Anti-Defamation League, told the City Club that violence in the Middle East along with worldwide economic distress have combined to produce "the biggest explosion of anti-Semitism globally that we have witnessed since World War II." Foxman said Israel's assault on Gaza was a response to Hamas rocket attacks on southern Israel and "as close to a just war as you can possibly have."

JUNE 5

JULY 10

### Frances Beinecke

Combating global climate change and reviving the U.S. economy are intertwined, said Frances Beinecke, president of the Natural Resources Defense Council. "The good news is that by investing in clean energy we can get our economy moving again, increase our national security, and protect our environment." Passage of climate-change legislation, then pending in Congress, she said, "frames the solution with the United States in the lead."

### Aneesh Chopra

Aneesh Chopra, recently tapped by President Barack Obama to become the nation's first chief technology officer, said more practical applications need to be developed so individuals see the value of having high-speed network connections. "Give people the reason to use the technology, and they will run like the wind," he said. Congress has put billions of dollars toward technology initiatives as part of its wide-reaching stimulus package, including $7.2 billion for broadband infrastructure improvement.

**Victor Rivers**, actor, author, and spokesman for the National Network to End Domestic Violence

**Joe Solmonese**, president of the Human Rights Campaign of the United States

**Cardinal Francis Arinze**, an Igbo Nigerian and the Cardinal Bishop of Velletri-Segni (the office vacated by the ascension of Cardinal Ratzinger to the papacy)

**Gen. George Casey Jr.**, chief of staff of the United States Army

## Representative John A. Boehner
August 24, 2010

Declaring that Washington is "tired, broken, and bloated," Representative John A. Boehner of Ohio, House Republican leader, delivered a measured but forceful speech denouncing President Barack Obama's economic policies and putting forth his own ideas to revitalize the economy.

After being elected to Congress in 1990, Boehner quickly established himself as a voice for reform. He adopted a "no earmarks" policy, was part of the Gang of Seven that brought media attention to the House banking and Congressional Post Office scandals, and in 1994 joined Representative Newt Gingrich in crafting the Republican Contract with America, a galvanizing platform that helped his party win majority control of Congress in 1994 for the first time in four decades.

The economy, Boehner said, is "stalled by stimulus spending and hamstrung by uncertainty and the prospect of higher taxes and more regulation."

"When I travel around the state," Boehner said, "I talk to employers, who are not only trying to create jobs but just trying to keep the people they have on the payroll." Members of Congress, he told the City Club, don't think about the fact that the employees of a small business are like members of a family whose "bonds have been frayed by a struggling economy." Employers, the organizer of a job fair in Columbus told him, "are scared to death."

A month earlier, Boehner said, he had conveyed to the president that the ongoing uncertainty is hurting small business and preventing the creation of private-sector jobs. Not long after they spoke, the president signed a $26 billion stimulus spending bill that funnels money to the states to protect government jobs. "Even worse, it's funded by a new tax that makes it more expensive to create jobs here in the United States and less expensive to create jobs overseas. This cannot continue. I've had enough, and I think that the American people have had enough."

Boehner proposed five actions that the president should take immediately "to break this economic uncertainty and help more Americans find an honest day's work":

1. The president should announce that he will not carry out his plan to impose "job-killing tax hikes" on families and small businesses. "Raising taxes on families and small businesses during a recession is a recipe for disaster—for both our economy and our deficit."

2. The president should announce that he will veto any "job-killing bill" sent to his desk by a lame-duck Congress—including a national energy tax and the "card-check bill," which would eliminate the right of non-union workers to a secret ballot.

3. The president should call on Democratic leaders in Congress "to stop obstructing Republican attempts to repeal the new health care law's job-killing 1099 mandate" [under which companies would have to report the purchase of any item costing more than $600].[8] The president's "takeover" of health care, he said, "is wreaking havoc on employers."

4. The president should submit to Congress an "aggressive spending-reduction package" that cuts non-defense spending to 2008 levels. "This would show," Boehner said, "that Washington is serious about bringing down the deficit." He added, "All the stimulus spending has gotten us nowhere."

> "Virtually no one in the White House has run a small business or created jobs in the private sector."

8. On April 14, 2011, President Barack Obama signed a bill repealing the 1099 tax-compliance mandate in the health care law.

**"We've run out of road to kick the bucket down."**

5. The president should ask for the resignations of his economic team, including Treasury Secretary Timothy F. Geithner and Lawrence Summers [director of the White House's National Economic Council]. Employers and small-business owners, he charged, are "rightly frustrated" that no one is listening to them. "Virtually no one in the White House," Boehner said, "has run a small business or created jobs in the private sector"—a lack that shows in the policies coming out of the administration.

"Our fresh start begins now," the Republican leader said, directing his listeners to the website of America Speaking Out, where "thousands of ideas are percolating" that will lead to a new agenda for the nation.

"I have said that if I were fortunate enough to be the Speaker of the House," Boehner said, "I would run the House differently—differently from Republicans and Democrats." He derided the extension of unemployment insurance as "irresponsible" and again pounded "job-killing tax hikes," asking, "Is it right to force our kids and grandkids to pay for this?" By trying and failing to build a recovery on government stimulus spending, Boehner said, Washington "has kept the private sector in bust while the public sector has had a boom." Federal workers, Boehner charged, now make more than private-sector workers, and the president has "191 new regulations in the queue."

"Instead of growing Big Government, let's focus on growing small businesses around our country," said Boehner. "For twenty years now I've watched leaders in both parties look at the big issues, the tough issues, and then I watched them look away. Now we're just out of time. We've run out of road to kick the bucket down. It's time to put the grown-ups in charge."

© 2010 DONN R. NOTTAGE

MAY 3

JUNE 18

AUGUST 27

**Christina Romer**

Noting that Ohio has hit
11 percent unemployment
as the state has lost more
than 400,000 jobs since the
recession started, Christina
Romer, chair of President
Barack Obama's Council
of Economic Advisers, told
the City Club she remains
optimistic about the future
of manufacturing-heavy
areas like Northeast Ohio.

**Richard Trumka**

Richard Trumka, president
of the AFL-CIO, said
his organization supports
immigration reform because
current laws and policies
have created a permanent
underclass of undocumented
workers open to exploitation
by employers. "Too many
employers like a system
where our borders are
closed and opened at the
same time—closed enough
to turn immigrants into
second-class citizens, open
enough to ensure an endless
supply of socially and legally
powerless cheap labor," he
said.

**Adm. Mike Mullen**

With the last combat troops
in Iraq on their way home,
Admiral Mike Mullen,
chairman of the Joint Chiefs
of Staff, said it's time for
America's communities to
step up and help returning
veterans transition back
to the civilian world.
Mullen spoke as part of a
three-day tour to promote
the establishment of
community resources that
former military personnel
can tap to assist them with
obtaining jobs, education,
and vet-to-vet mentoring.
He described returning vets
as "a rich talent pool" and "a
generation geared to serve."

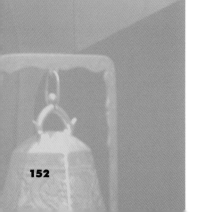

NOVEMBER 19

**Bill Adair**

Bill Adair, Washington Bureau chief of the *St. Petersburg Times* and editor of the national fact-check website PolitiFact, said political discourse too often is driven by the talking point. Politicians and party leaders, he said, are so programmed to "score points against the other side" that facts no longer matter, especially on cable news programs.

**Wayne LaPierre**, CEO and executive vice president, National Rifle Association

**Douglas A. Blackmon**, author of *Slavery by Another Name: The Re-Enslavement of Black Americans from the Civil War to World War II*

**Michael Roizen**, chief wellness officer, the Cleveland Clinic

**Ronn Richard**, president and CEO, the Cleveland Foundation

**Ted Gup**, author of *A Secret Gift: How One Man's Kindness—and a Trove of Letters—Revealed the Hidden History of the Great Depression*

# 2011

## Alan K. Simpson
November 18, 2011

Former Senator Alan K. Simpson, Republican of Wyoming, used his characteristic droll wit and plain speaking to good effect as he discussed his recent service as co-chair of the National Commission on Fiscal Responsibility and Reform (also known as the Simpson-Bowles Commission). Created by President Barack Obama in February 2010 to study the national debt crisis, the eighteen-member bipartisan panel was charged with "identifying policies to improve the fiscal situation in the medium term and to achieve fiscal sustainability over the long run."

"It took us four months just to establish trust," said Simpson, who served in the Senate from 1979 to 1997, much of that time as party leader. He described the fraught political atmosphere in which he, together with his co-chair, Erskine Bowles, a former chief of staff to President Bill Clinton, conducted their work.

"Critics on the far left complained, 'Erskine is not a real Democrat—he's a fake.' Those on the right called me 'a Republican toady covering Obama's fanny so he can destroy the Republican Party.' I've never seen such hostility, discord, and dysfunctional behavior between and among both parties," said Simpson with disgust. "It's very sad to witness. You can't succeed as a legislator unless you can work with those on the other side. You either learn how to compromise [on] an issue without compromising yourself or get out of the game."

> **"Critics on the far left complained, 'Erskine is not a real Democrat —he's a fake.' Those on the right called me 'a Republican toady covering Obama's fanny so he can destroy the Republican Party.'"**

Simpson vividly sketched the dimensions of the nation's fiscal problem. "Who's the biggest spending president in the history of the United States before this guy (meaning President Obama)?" he asked. "Answer: George W. Bush, who never vetoed a single spending bill, ran up the pharmacy bill[9] without a bit of money to pay for it, and fought two wars with no tax to support it. We've never had a war in our history that didn't have a tax to support it."

When the commission asked the defense department how many contractors it had, Simpson said, the answer was "we don't know—between one and ten million." Simpson added, "When President Eisenhower said beware of the military-industrial complex, we should have listened. The ties are deep, and they're opaque," he said ominously. He cited the lifetime health insurance benefits enjoyed by millions of veterans and their dependents, for which they pay $470 annually and which require no copay and no means-testing. The cost to the federal government: $53 billion last year alone. "I've had my head pounded in by the VFW, the American Legion, the DAV," Defense Secretary Robert Gates told him, "You take it on."

"So Erskine and I just kept prowling around [for cost savings] . . . We just kept pushing," said Simpson. "We feel we have actually reached the ultimate plan. We have succeeded beautifully because we have effectively pissed off everyone in America."

To spell out the problem, Simpson said, he doesn't need charts or PowerPoint. "If you spend more than you earn, you lose your butt. If you spend a buck and borrow 41 cents of it, you have to be stupid. Your country, this day, is borrowing $3,800,000,000. And we'll do it tomorrow and the next day and the next, ad infinitum."

One hundred and four different interest groups testified before the commission, Simpson said, each one pleading, "Don't touch us." On the Social Security system, Simpson said he's had a "bellyful" of complaints, with "the nastiest, most vicious letters" coming from people over seventy. Social Security, he reminded the City Club audience, "was never, ever intended as a retirement [plan]. It was an income *supplement*." He went on to excoriate the American Association of Retired Persons (AARP) for its intransigence, saying, "There's been no shared sacrifice in this country since World War II." Calling health care "the biggest mastodon in the kitchen," he said Medicare and Medicaid "are out of whack and unworkable."

The United States, Simpson concluded, "is in extremity. We owe fifteen trillion dollars." Then, speaking slowly and carefully enunciating each word, he issued a warning: "If this country is in thrall to the AARP and to Grover Norquist,[10] we haven't got a prayer."

In the question and answer period, Simpson was asked about the president's response to the commission's final report.[11] "The president knew that if he approved it he would be torn to shreds," Simpson said, adding, "Now [he's] in full election mode." On the subject of a polarized and dysfunctional Congress, Simpson said, "If Grover Norquist is the most powerful person in America today—and I think he is—then he should run for president. But don't forget, Grover can't murder you. He can't burn down your house. The only thing he can do is defeat you for re-election. And if that means more to you than your country in extremity, when we need patriots, you shouldn't be in Congress."

> "We've never had a war in our history that didn't have a tax to support it."

9. After passing Congress by a narrow margin, the Medicare Prescription Drug, Improvement, and Modernization Act was signed into law by President George W. Bush on December 8, 2003.

10. Grover Norquist, a founder and president of Americans for Tax Reform, is known as the promoter of the "Taxpayer Protection Pledge" by which candidates and incumbents commit themselves to oppose any and all tax increases.

11. Support for the plan fell three votes short of the 14-vote supermajority required to send the package to Congress.

MARCH 17

APRIL 2

JULY 15

### Michelle Rhee

Michelle Rhee, the former chancellor of the Washington, D.C., school district, described the qualities needed by the next leader of the Cleveland public schools, including a clear vision, the ability to manage people through change, tough skin, and "fire in the belly." During her three years at the helm of the District's schools, Rhee became a target for critics who faulted her decisions to close underperforming schools and to fire teachers deemed ineffective. "We did make tremendous academic gains," Rhee said, "but still fell far short of our expectations of where we wanted our kids to be."

### Nancy Brinker

The founder and CEO of Susan G. Komen for the Cure, Nancy Brinker, told the City Club about her twenty-eight years as head of the largest and best-funded breast cancer organization in the United States. A former U.S. ambassador to Hungary and chief of protocol during the last two years of former President George W. Bush's first term, Brinker said that over the next few years Komen will focus on improving survival outcomes for minority women, whose mortality rates have not declined at the same rates as those of white women.

### Dr. Margaret A. Hamburg

Food and Drug Administration Commissioner Margaret A. Hamburg told the City Club that her agency will launch an initiative to boost innovation and speed up the medical products pipeline. Hamburg acknowledged that innovations have been hindered by the costs associated with the FDA's regulatory process, which is more complicated than the one followed in Europe, and promised that the agency will work to streamline it.

OCTOBER 24

**Jim Thome**
Cleveland Indians slugger
Jim Thome fielded questions
from the team's radio voice,
Tom Hamilton, then from
the capacity audience.
Thome, a fan favorite who
joined the Indians in 1991
and holds the baseball
team's all-time records for
career home runs (334) and
homers in a season (52), had
left for Philadelphia as a free
agent after the 2002 season
but returned in late August
2011 for the final few weeks
of the season.

**Johanna Orozco**, teen
educator, Domestic Violence
& Child Advocacy Center
of Greater Cleveland

**Aimee Mullins**, athlete,
actress, and fashion model
whose legs were amputated
below the knee at age
one due to the congenital
absence of her lower leg
bones and who learned to
walk and run, at record-
setting speed, on flexible
prosthetic legs

**Steve and Cokie
Roberts**, husband-and-wife
journalists and authors of
*From This Day Forward*

**Isabel Wilkerson**,
Pulitzer Prize-winning
journalist and author of *The
Warmth of Other Suns: The
Epic Story of America's Great
Migration*

**Scott Cowen**, president of
Tulane University, named
by *Time* magazine as one
of the nation's Top 10 Best
College Presidents

# 2012

The billionaire media mogul appeared before the City Club to accept the club's Citadel of Free Speech Award. Ted Turner was recognized as the founder, in 1976, of the Turner Broadcasting System (TBS), the nation's first "superstation" and, in 1980, Cable News Network (CNN), the world's first 24-hour all-news television channel. Turner, said City Club President Hugh McKay, "has dramatically expanded the scope and breadth of cable television and has done much to facilitate the exercise of free speech . . . and to catalyze the discussion of issues of global importance." After graciously accepting the award, Turner sat down for an interview with nationally syndicated columnist Connie Shultz and then took questions from the audience. Turner was open and engaging throughout the hour.

"So, Ted Turner," Schultz began, "when was the last time you were here in Cleveland?" Turner himself had planted the question. He responded, "1995, when the Braves and the Indians . . ." He got no further, the capacity crowd erupting with laughter at the reminder that Turner's Atlanta Braves had, in six close games, won the World Series that year over the Cleveland Indians.

Schultz asked about Turner's childhood, which, he acknowledged in his book *Call Me Ted*, had been a painful one. Born in Cincinnati, he was sent off to boarding school at four, to military school at nine. He suffered from abandonment, he said, and admitted that to this day he does not like to be alone.

Turner said he did a lot of reading as a boy, especially about nature and the environment. "I was an environmentalist at the age of ten," he said. He also enjoyed history. "I was interested in what made people do things, why empires rose and fell, why some people were successful and others weren't," he said, adding, "because I wanted to be successful."

The conversation turned to politics. Turner said his father, a potent figure in his life, believed in "my country right or wrong" and told him, "All businessmen are Republicans." Turner, however, gravitated left politically and has put much of his wealth to work for environmental and humanitarian causes. In 2001, he founded the Nuclear Threat Initiative, a foundation working to eliminate global threats from nuclear, biological, and chemical weapons. "The only thing to do is get rid of them," he said. In 1997, Turner announced a pledge of $1 billion to the United Nations Foundation, whose four core priorities are women and population, children's health, the environment, and peace and security. "Giving equal rights to women," Turner said, "segues to [control of] population explosion and hunger . . . There are 250 million women in the world who would use birth control if they had it. What I'm working on is survival of the human race and life on earth."

Asked what he thinks about the state of television journalism today, Turner said, "Some's good, some's bad," admitting "I don't watch much television." When he does, he watches CNN, adding, "I'd like to see them do more international news and more serious news and less who-murdered-who. Every day it's the 'murder of the day.'"

During the first Gulf War (1990–1991), CNN pioneered live coverage from the front lines of the battle. In the lead-up to war, Turner said, "Some thought we should stay, some thought we should leave. If you're a war correspondent, you're a war correspondent. Two [journalists] volunteered to go." Later, on the eve of war in Iraq, he said, "They didn't have anybody who wanted to go. I called them up . . . and told them I would go. They said,

> "I don't like the United Nations—I *love* the United Nations. And I'm absolutely convinced that if we had not had the U.N., we'd already have had World War III and we'd all be dead."

'You don't have enough experience.'" Turner shrugged, drawing laughter when he added, "All you do is stand there and [ducking his head as if reacting to an incoming missile] 'Wow, that was close.'"

During the question-and-answer period, Turner, who owns two million acres of land in twelve states, expanded on his interest in conservation. As a little boy, he said, he read about the bison and learned that there were some thirty million here at the time of Columbus. By 1972, when he started to raise bison, he said, they were on the verge of extinction. "I went from 3 to 56,000 now . . . along with all the other wildlife. We don't even kill rattlesnakes or prairie dogs," he said. Turner said he uses no pesticides on his land, which he blamed for the demise of songbirds. "To see us mismanaging our planet the way that we are breaks my heart," he said. "Prairie dogs have been just as exterminated as the bison. The smallest, the largest—doesn't matter, we'll kill anything, and I'm sick of it. And I'm trying to do something about it, what little I can."

Asked his opinion of the IPO for Facebook, he shrugged his shoulders and drolly said, "People used to buy Eastman Kodak too . . . Don't ask me—I lost $8 billion merging [Time Warner] with AOL." The audience laughed heartily.

On the United Nations, which some have criticized for its inability to handle international conflicts, Turner was outspoken. "I don't like the United Nations—I *love* the United Nations," he said. "And I'm absolutely convinced that if we had not had the U.N., we'd already have had World War III and we'd all be dead." Replying to other questions, Turner expressed disgust with a dysfunctional Congress and support for public financing of political campaigns and clean energy. "We need to phase out fossil fuel as soon as we can," he said.

Turner named his father as the greatest influence in his life. But by age fifty Ed Turner had achieved his goals and, with nothing to live for and suffering from depression, took his own life. Ed Turner had once advised his son, "'Set your goals so high that you can't possibly accomplish them.' So I did—saving the world . . ." Turner broke off and slowly rolled his head, amused by his own little joke.

CITY CLUB VIDEO

© 2010 DONN R. NOTTAGE

JANUARY 13          JANUARY 18          MAY 4

### Grover Norquist

Grover Norquist, the founder and president of Americans for Tax Reform, defended the "Taxpayer Protection Pledge" his organization has been asking candidates to sign since the 1980s. While some blame the pledge for Congress's inability to reach consensus on national spending issues, Norquist sees a principled stand against higher taxes. "The pledge is what makes tax reform possible, because Americans can trust Congress to go into a dark room and not raise taxes," he said.

### Steven Chu

Declaring that the U.S. has the intellectual fire power to surpass technological and engineering research done in any other nation, U.S. Secretary of Energy Steven Chu said the government has a policy role to play through the purchase of new technological projects and must continue to finance research because China is doing it. "America has reached a crossroads and faces a stark decision. Do we play to win in the clean-energy race, creating U.S. jobs by making and selling clean-energy technologies, or do we bow out and follow our dependence on foreign oil with a dependence on foreign solar panels and wind turbines?"

### Valerie Jarrett

Valerie Jarrett, a senior advisor to President Barack Obama, credited the administration for a record accomplished despite "an unprecedented level of gridlock." Jarrett pointed to twenty-six consecutive months of job growth, passage of the Dodd-Frank Wall Street Reform and Consumer Protection Act, initiatives to reduce oil imports, and improved veterans' benefits. She added that the president is "moving forward" with a plan to end the war in Afghanistan after he brings the Iraq war to a "responsible end."

OCTOBER 12

**Enda Kenny**
The Republic of Ireland is on an economic upswing, Prime Minister Enda Kenny told the City Club. Despite unemployment above 14 percent, Kenny said exports are up and high-tech industries are flowering, thanks to an uptick in investments by U.S. companies, including the Cleveland Clinic, at whose main campus Kenny spoke.

**Sr. Carol Keehan**, a member of the Daughters of Charity of Saint Vincent de Paul and the president and CEO of the Catholic Health Association

**Diane Ravitch**, research professor of education at New York University and a historian of education

**Irshad Manji**, a Canadian professor, advocate for the reform of traditional Islam, and author of *Allah, Liberty and Love: The Courage to Reconcile Faith and Freedom*

# Historical Timeline of the City Club of Cleveland

**June 14, 1912**
Mayo Fesler, secretary of the Municipal Association, and Augustus R. Hatton, a professor of political science at Western Reserve University, call together a number of civic-minded young men for lunch at the Chamber of Commerce building. Those present hear addresses by representatives of the city clubs of Chicago, Boston, and St. Louis, and appoint a committee of ten to study and report on the advisability of establishing such a club in Cleveland.

**July 30, 1912**
The committee recommends the organization of a city club "which will furnish a common meeting place for citizens of Cleveland who are interested in public questions; and a wider forum for the free and general discussion of civic, social, political and economic questions of general interest."

**October 28, 1912**
The City Club of Cleveland is incorporated under the laws of Ohio. Two days later, at the first meeting of the City Club, 104 men agree to buy $10 shares in the new corporation. Newton D. Baker emphasizes the need for the club to maintain a nonpartisan spirit to facilitate the unbiased discussion of public matters.

**November 25, 1912**
The *Cleveland Plain Dealer* reports the results of the first City Club election: Daniel E. Morgan, president; Edward M. Baker, vice president; Amasa Stone Mather, treasurer. The officers ask Mayo Fesler to continue temporarily as secretary.

**December 21, 1912**
The first City Club Forum features a talk by Brand Whitlock, the reform mayor of Toledo. The remaining forums of the club's first season address topics of local government. There is also a presentation on child labor by the social worker Florence Kelley, to which women guests are invited.

**May 1913**
The City Club establishes its clubrooms on the third floor of Weber's restaurant, 244 Superior Avenue. The club's dining room occupies the second floor, where daily noonday luncheons are enjoyed by club members, who engage in lively discussions of politics and current events.

**1914**
The City Club puts on its first "stunt night," a musical-comedy satire taking aim at local politics and politicians. "Stunt night" soon evolves to become the Anvil Revue, written, acted, and staged by club members. Carl D. Friebolin, federal bankruptcy referee, serves as the longtime writer and director of the annual show, which lampoons political bigwigs and anyone else who deserves skewering.

**1916**
Ralph A. Hayes, the club's first paid secretary, pens "The Creed of the City Club," which reads in part, "I hail and harbor and hear men of every belief and party . . . I have a forum—as wholly uncensored as it is rigidly impartial. 'Freedom of Speech' is graven above my rostrum . . ."

**September 21, 1916**
The City Club moves to more spacious accommodations, occupying the third floor of a new addition to the Hollenden Hotel at the corner of East Sixth Street and Vincent Avenue. The lease grants the club use of the hotel ballroom for its forums. Francis T. "Pat" Hayes is named club secretary. During his seven-year tenure, membership grows to 2,500.

**1921**
Secretary Hayes reports that during 1920 the City Club held 46 forum programs with a total attendance of 30,925. This number—a record—includes forums conducted by the club's "forum extension committee" at the Goodrich Social Settlement, East Technical High School, and Public Square.

**December 16, 1928**
A talk titled "The Friendly Arctic" by the explorer and ethnologist Vilhjalmur Stefansson marks the start of regular live radio broadcasts of the City Club Forum over station WHK.

**November 12, 1929**
The City Club dedicates its new home at 712 Vincent Avenue. The two-story clubhouse features a large high-ceilinged dining room on the ground floor, with a lounge, recreation rooms, and offices above. The Anvil Revue is produced at Cleveland's Music Hall before an audience of more than two thousand.

**1931**
With the onset of the Depression, the City Club suffers financial losses but survives, in large measure thanks to Jack J. Lafferty, appointed club secretary this year. Lafferty will serve until 1957.

**1940**

The City Club Forum Foundation is established. The foundation gives non-members, women, and radio listeners, as well as club members, a way to support the weekly forums. The first large gift comes from Congresswoman Frances Payne Bolton in memory of her late husband, Chester C. Bolton, a longtime member of the City Club.

Live radio broadcast of the City Club Forum moves to WGAR.

**October 10, 1942**

Artist Rockwell Kent opens the new season of the City Club Forum, at which the club dedicates *Freedom of Speech*, a mural depicting the democratic spirit of the City Club. The mural is the work of the Cleveland artist Elmer W. Brown, an African American.

**1961**

The City Club launches a public campaign to raise $150,000 for the City Club Forum Foundation. City Club stalwart Philip W. Porter uses his *Plain Dealer* column to call attention to the drive, writing, "The fees and expenses for speakers have gone higher and higher each year. Those provocative and prominent people you listen to on WGAR Saturdays command, and get, the going rate for speaking. It's not hay."

**1964**

The City Club moves its weekly forum from Saturday to Friday. "[The] reason is obvious," Mary Hirschfield writes in the *Plain Dealer*. "It's very difficult to get any kind of a crowd downtown on Saturdays."

**April 5, 1968**

One day after the assassination of Martin Luther King Jr., Senator Robert F. Kennedy, in his quest for the Democratic presidential nomination, is scheduled to address the City Club at the Hotel Sheraton Cleveland. He discards his planned speech and instead makes a few brief remarks, telling a somber audience, "This is a time of shame and sorrow. It is not a day for politics."

**October 1970**

Live radio broadcasts of the City Club Forum move to WCLV.

**March 16, 1971**

Alan J. Davis is named executive director of the City Club.

**July 1971**

The City Club moves to the Women's Federal Savings & Loan building, 320 Superior Avenue, where it shares some facilities, including a kitchen, with the Women's City Club. The combined headquarters is known as the "Cleveland Civic House."

**February 16, 1972**

Thomas F. Campbell (in favor) and James B. Davis (against) debate the admission of women to membership in the City Club. Those in attendance vote 65 to 63 in favor of admitting women, but passage requires a two-thirds majority. Three months later, the club schedules another vote. "The choice," City Club President Larry Robinson tells the *Plain Dealer*, "is whether the members want to perpetuate a men's eating club or a club with a social function of presenting public debate." On June 2, another vote is taken, and club members vote 228 to 97 to admit women.

**1972**

Bertram E. Gardner, vice president of urban affairs for the Cleveland Trust Company, becomes the first African American to be elected president of the City Club.

**October 28, 1972**

The City Club turns 60, marking the year with an "unprecedented" lineup of speakers, including Senator and presidential candidate George S. McGovern; R. Sargent Shriver, his running mate; former U.S. Attorney General and Secretary of the Treasury George P. Schulz; Leonard Woodcock, president of the UAW; L. Patrick Gray, chief of the FBI; George H. W. Bush, U.S. ambassador to the UN; and Russell Means, national coordinator for the American Indian Movement. Executive Director Alan Davis tells the *Cleveland Press* that he has searched the files and "there's never been a forum season quite like this one."

**1973**

The first women members are elected to the board of directors: Rena Blumberg, community affairs director for WIXY-WDOK, and Vilma Kohn, an attorney with Squire, Sanders & Dempsey.

**1976**

Owing to declining interest, the City Club abandons its annual Anvil Revue. Alan Davis tells the *Cleveland Press*, "Perhaps it has just outlived its time."

**1978**

Trustees elect attorney Annette G. Butler, an African American, president the City Club. She is the first woman to serve in the position.

**1980**
WCLV begins distributing City Club Forums of national interest to National Public Radio stations around the country. Eventually, over one hundred stations will carry the programs.

**1982**
Trustees of the City Club and the Women's City Club vote to relocate to the second floor of the Citizens Building, 850 Euclid Avenue.

**1983**
The City Club and Women's City Club host one thousand members and friends at an opening reception in their new quarters.

**1985**
The City Club establishes a Hall of Fame to honor members who have made significant contributions to the club. The first four to be elected are Daniel E. Morgan, legislator, city manager, judge, city reformer, and first president of the City Club; Peter Witt, trade unionist and member of Mayor Tom L. Johnson's cabinet; Carl D. Friebolin, federal bankruptcy referee and the longtime creator, writer, and producer of the City Club's Anvil Revue; and Philip W. Porter, retired executive editor of the *Plain Dealer* and a founder of the City Club Forum Foundation.

**October 28, 1987**
The City Club marks its 75th anniversary in spectacular fashion. With broad corporate sponsorship, the "Power of Ideas" celebration features a banquet at the Stouffer Tower City Plaza Hotel with a host of nationally prominent guest speakers, including Mario Cuomo, Phil Donohue, John Kenneth Galbraith, Jeane Kirkpatrick, Eleanor Holmes Norton, T. Boone

Pickens, and Gloria Steinem. As part of its anniversary celebration, the City Club establishes a program of endowed forums to assure the continuity of its widely respected forums. Longtime City Club member Stanley I. Adelstein, a Cleveland attorney, spearheads the hugely successful effort to recruit donors.

**1993**
James H. Foster is named managing director of the City Club. Two years later, he is named executive director, replacing Alan Davis, who retires.

**1998**
The City Club gives its first Citadel of Free Speech Award to Senator John Glenn, Democrat of Ohio.

**1999**
The City Club embarks on a $2.5 million capital campaign to raise money for its endowment and finance the major renovation of its entire facility.

**2005**
The City Club board adopts a strategic plan, vowing to improve the diversity of its membership and forum attendance, take greater advantage of technology to expand the distribution of its programs, and strengthen the national reputation that draws remarkable speakers to its podium.

**2008**
Radio broadcasts of the City Club Forum move to WCPN.

**2011**
The City Club boasts thirty-three endowed forums, presented annually and in perpetuity, on such themes as civil liberties, health care, the environment, local politics, and cultural arts.

**2011–2012**
The City Club marks its centennial year with a National Conference on Free Speech, a free speech essay competition for area high school students, and an encore speaker series, culminating in the "Power of Ideas²" centennial celebration at the Renaissance Cleveland Hotel on October 18, 2012.

**April 15, 2013**
Dan Moulthrop is named chief executive officer of the City Club.

# Presidents of the City Club of Cleveland

| | | | | | |
|---|---|---|---|---|---|
| 1912–13 | Daniel E. Morgan | 1949 | Hugh Kane | 1985 | William J. Woestendiek |
| 1914 | Edward M. Baker | 1950 | Harold J. Glickman | 1986 | Robert M. Lustig |
| 1915 | Erie C. Hopwood | 1951 | Charles L. Lawrence | 1987 | David I. Sindell |
| 1916 | Augustus R. Hatton | 1952 | John B. Mullaney | 1988 | Dennis J. Dooley |
| 1917 | George W. York | 1953 | Julian Griffin | 1989 | Elisabeth T. Dreyfuss |
| 1918 | Carl D. Friebolin | 1954 | Henry W. Hopwood | 1990 | Chester J. Gray |
| 1919 | Allard Smith | 1955 | Stanley P. Barnett | 1991 | Frederick I. Taft |
| 1920 | John D. Fackler | 1956 | Ralph E. Crow | 1992 | Scott C. Finerman |
| 1921 | Wallace M. Pattison | 1957 | Thomas L. Boardman | 1993 | Howard C. Landau |
| 1922 | Winfred G. Leutner | 1958 | Everest P. Derthick | 1994 | Steven R. Smith |
| 1923 | Frank C. Cain | 1959 | William S. Burton | 1995 | Sheldon L. Braverman |
| 1924 | Robert J. Bulkley | 1960 | Howard B. Klein | 1996 | Arthur V. N. Brooks |
| 1925 | Joel B. Hayden | 1961 | Robert H. Rawson | 1997 | Njeri Nuru-Holm |
| 1926 | A. H. Throckmorton | 1962 | Samuel O. Freedlander | 1998 | Richard W. Pogue |
| 1927 | Charles H. Lake | 1963 | Barton R. Clausen | 1999 | Brian D. Tucker |
| 1928 | William A. Stinchcomb | 1964 | Donald S. Carmichael | 2000 | Anthony C. Peebles |
| 1929 | Edward W. Doty | 1865 | Peter DiLeone | 2001 | Leonard M. Calabrese |
| 1930 | John J. Thomas | 1966 | Sidney Andorn | 2002 | Claire Rosacco |
| 1931 | Charles W. Sellers | 1967 | Richard Campbell | 2003 | Steve D. Bullock |
| 1932 | Ted Robinson | 1968 | Russell M. Kane | 2004 | Kevin J. Donahue |
| 1933 | Russell Weisman | 1969 | Milton Widder | 2005 | Sanjiv K. Kapur |
| 1934 | Marcellus DeVaughn | 1970 | Thomas F. Campbell | 2006 | Courtney S. DeOreo |
| 1935 | John W. Barkley | 1971 | Craig Spangenberg | 2007 | Lee Friedman |
| 1936 | Paul Bellamy | 1972 | Larry Robinson | 2008 | Ralph Della Ratta Jr. |
| 1937 | Henry M. Busch | 1973 | Bertram Gardner | 2009 | Jan L. Roller |
| 1938 | George B. Harris | 1974 | Sidney Josephs | 2010 | Paul N. Harris |
| 1939 | Marc J. Grossman | 1975 | Kiely Cronin | 2011 | Hugh E. McKay |
| 1940 | Philip W. Porter | 1976 | Robert R. Cavano | 2012 | Hewitt Shaw |
| 1941 | Nathaniel R. Howard | 1977 | David L. Hoehnen | 2013 | Paul N. Harris |
| 1942 | Albert I. Cornsweet | 1978 | Robert Bry | | |
| 1943 | Richard T. F. Harding | 1979 | Annette Butler | | |
| 1944 | Edward Blythin | 1980 | James Lipscomb | | |
| 1945 | Wilbur A. White | 1981 | Herb Kamm | | |
| 1946 | Wendell A. Falsgraf | 1982 | Nelson E. Weiss | | |
| 1947 | Spencer D. Irwin | 1983 | Nancy C. Cronin | | |
| 1948 | Mark C. Schinnerer | 1984 | James I. Huston | | |

## Chief Executives of the
## City Club of Cleveland

| | |
|---|---|
| 1912–1915 | Mayo Fesler |
| 1915–1916 | Ralph A. Hayes |
| 1916–1923 | Francis T. Hayes* |
| 1923–1931 | Charles B. Ryan |
| 1931–1957 | John J. "Jack" Lafferty |
| 1957–1959 | James M. Davenport |
| 1959–1965 | William E. Sanborn |
| 1965–1968 | Peter B. Halbin |
| 1968–1971 | Frederick A. Vierow |
| 1971–1994 | Alan J. Davis |
| 1994–2013 | James H. Foster |
| 2013– | Dan Moulthrop |

*includes military service during the
First World War

## A Note on Sources

This essay depended substantially on back issues of the *Cleveland Plain Dealer*, to date the only one of the city's major newspapers to be digitized. The *Plain Dealer* reported frequently on the City Club's activities and, until recent years, carried detailed accounts of most City Club Forums. Other sources included personal interviews with longtime club members (named in the Preface and Acknowledgements); the Cleveland Press Collection in the Michael Schwartz Library of Cleveland State University; *The City*, a weekly newsletter of the City Club of Cleveland published from 1915 until 2013; various City Club annual reports; and miscellaneous secondary sources published by or about the City Club listed below, all of which can be found in the collections of the Cleveland Public Library.

Campbell, Thomas F. *Freedom's Forum: The City Club 1912–1962*. Cleveland: The City Club, 1962.

City Club of Cleveland. *The City Club . . . a Civilized Idea*. Cleveland: City Club of Cleveland, 1936.

____. *The City Club of Cleveland, Dedication and Opening of the City Club's New Home, 712 Vincent Avenue, Tuesday, November 12th, 1929.*

____. *The Crossroads of Cleveland*. Cleveland: City Club of Cleveland, 1930.

Gottlieb, Mark and Diana Tittle. *America's Soapbox: Seventy-five Years of Free Speaking at Cleveland's City Club Forum*. Cleveland: Citizens Press, 1987.

Raper, John W. *The Soviet Table, or The Rise of Civilization in Cleveland*. Cleveland: Public Affairs Committee of Cuyahoga County, 1935.

# Index of Names

Abercrombie-Winstanley, Gina, 129

Abzug, Bella, 31

Adair, Bill, 153

Adams, Gerry, 89

Addams, Jane, 10

Adelstein, Hope, 40n13, 51

Adelstein, Stanley I., 3, 40, 40n13, 51, 52

Akers, Bruce, 42, 44, 45

Albright, Madeleine, 49, 128

Alburn, John A., 4

Allen, Florence E., 7, 7n3

Allende, Hortensia Bussi de, 37

Anderson, Jack, 38

Anderson, Lillian, 34–35, 44

Andorn, Sidney, 31

Arinze, Francis, 149

Ashkenazy, Vladimir, 101

Ashrawi, Hanan, 137

Baker, Edward M., 4

Baker, Newton D., 4, 5, 6, 8, 40

Baldwin, Arthur, 5

Bambrick, James J., 38

Bandar bin Sultan, 49, 125

Barbour, Haley, 93

Barr, Robert, 133

Barrie, Dennis, 73

Bassiouni, M. Cherif, 88

Beinecke, Frances, 149

Belding, Walter H., 18

Bellamy, Paul, 23

Bellamy, Peter, 18

Benchley, Robert, 11

Benesch, Alfred A., 6

Bennett, Floyd, 11

Berenbaum, Michael, 84

Bergman, Robert P., 93

Berrigan, Philip, 37

Biden, Joseph R., Jr., 37

Bieber, Owen, 85

Blackmon, Douglas A., 153

Block, Herbert L., 27

Bloomfield, Sarah, 113

Blossom, Dudley S., 12

Blumberg Olshansky, Rena, 34, 36, 41

Boehner, John A., 46, 150–51

Bollinger, Lee C., 117

Bolton, Bill, 46

Bolton, Chester C., 22, 23

Bolton, Frances P., 23

Bond, Julian, 108

Bonda, Ted, 38

Borowitz, Andy, 129

Bostwick, Robert, 46

Bourgeois, Roy, 113

Boyd, Jerry (F. X. Toole), 50

Boyle, Gregory, 84

Brady, Sarah, 97

Branch, Taylor, 72

Brazaitis, Tom, 113

Brennan, Christine, 140

Brill, Steven, 46, 109

Brinker, Nancy, 156

Broder, David S., 37, 40, 47, 57, 110–11

Brooks, Art, 46

Broun, Heywood, 11

Brower, David, 61

Brown, Claude, 40

Brown, Elmer W., 24, 47

Brown, George, 22

Brown, Jerry, 81

Brown, Sherrod, 137

Brzezinski, Zbigniew, 64

Buckley, William F., Jr., 38

Burke, Thomas A., 32

Burns, Ken, 141

Burry, John, Jr., 45

Bush, George H. W., 35–36, 39

Bush, George W., 3, 46, 134–35, 155

Butler, Annette G., 36

Byers, Ed, 9

Cadwallader, Starr, 6

Cain, Frank C., 9, 12

Calabrese, Leonard M., 47, 51

Caldera, Louis, 112

Caldicott, Helen, 105

Campbell, Joan Brown, 109

Campbell, Thomas F., 7, 8, 15, 30, 33, 33n11, 34, 38

Canada, Geoffrey, 138–39

Carter, Jimmy, 38

Casey, George, Jr., 149

Cavano, Bob, 38

Celebrezze, Anthony J., 32

Cerf, Vinton, 136

Chang, Iris, 105

Chavez, Cesar, 37, 61

Cheney, Dick, 77

Chertoff, Michael, 145

Chopra, Aneesh, 149

Chu, Steven, 160

Church, Frank, 38

Cisneros, Henry, 133

Clark, Ramsey, 35, 57, 77

Clarke, John H., 7

Clarke, Ray W., 39

Clift, Eleanor, 113

Clinton, Bill, 44, 46, 81, 86–87

Coffin, William Sloane, 39, 70–71
Cohen, Ben, 105
Collins, Francis S., 51, 96
Connelly, John H., 35
Conners, William Randall, 22
Conrad, Robert, 19
Cosgrove, Delos (Toby), 132
Cowen, Scott, 157
Craig, Gregory B., 112
Cronin, Kiely, 34
Cronin, Nancy, 34
Cuomo, Mario, 41

Danaceau, Saul S., 20
Darrow, Clarence, 11
Daschle, Tom, 49, 124
Dash, Leon, 69
Davidson, Jo Ann, 93
Davis, Alan J., 19, 31, 34, 35, 42, 44, 50
Davis, Harry L., 7
Davis, James B., 33
Davis, William J., 64
Dawidowicz, Lucy, 40
Debs, Eugene V., 12, 12n6
DeCrow, Karen, 37
De Valera, Éamon, 10
DeWine, Mike, 137
Dickey, Nancy W., 108
DiLeone, Peter, 19, 41
Dohnányi, Christoph von, 72
Doll, Hank, 46
Donahue, Phil, 41
Donahue, Thomas R., 69
Dooley, Dennis, 34, 40, 41
Doty, Ed, 9

Dove, Rita, 98–99
Downie, Leonard, Jr., 120
Du Bois, W. E. B., 7, 24
Dunlop, Joan, 89
Durant, Will, 11

Eaton, Cyrus S., 27, 31
Edelman, Marian Wright, 102–3
Edwards, Elizabeth, 49, 140
Elders, M. Joycelyn, 88
Emanuel, Ezekial, 145

Fager, Jeffrey, 51
Falwell, Jerry, 39
Feagler, Dick, 69
Feather, William, 57
Fesler, Mayo, 4, 6, 7, 21
Firor, John, 68
Fisher, Antwone, 124
Florida, Richard, 49, 120
Flory, Walter L., 4
Fonda, Jane, 37
Forbes, George L., 43
Foster, Jim, 44, 45, 46, 47, 48, 49, 50, 51, 52
Foxman, Abraham, 148
Frampton, Eleanor, 18
Frank, Barney, 133
Frick, Ford, 26
Friebolin, Carl D., 6, 8, 10, 16–19, 23, 25
Friedan, Betty, 30, 39
Friendly, Fred, 37
Frist, Bill, 132
Fuller, Millard, 101

Galbraith, John Kenneth, 27, 37, 41
Gallup, George, 15
Gandhi, Rajmohan, 145
Gardner, Bertram E., 36
Garfield, James R., 7, 7n4
Gates, Henry Louis, Jr., 98–99
Gerard, Leo, 129
Gerberding, Julie, 132
Gettelfinger, Ron, 144
Gibson, David, 9
Gilder, George, 77
Ging, John, 148
Gingrich, Newt, 51, 90–91
Glenn, John, 73, 122–23
Glickman, Harold J., 18, 19
Goldsmith, A. M., 12
Goldstone, Steven F., 104
Gompers, Samuel, 10
Good, Mary Lowe, 69
Graham, Frank P., 28
Grasselli-Brown, Jeanette, 121
Gray, L. Patrick, III, 35
Gregory, Dick, 39
Gries, Moses J., 5
Guccione, Robert, 77
Gumbleton, Thomas J., 38
Gup, Ted, 117, 153
Guttmacher, Alan F., 27

Hall, Tex G., 137
Hamburg, Margaret A., 156
Hamid, Mohsin, 145
Hammer, Armand, 38
Hampton, Henry E., 65
Harding, Jack, 11
Harrington, Michael, 65
Harris, Louis, 81

Hatton, Augustus R., 4, 5, 7
Hawken, Paul, 92
Hayes, Francis T., 8, 9, 12
Hayes, Ralph A., 8, 25, 53
Hayes, Randall, 73
Healy, Bernadine, 85
Hegemann, Werner, 7
Henry, Frederick A., 5
Herbert, Thomas J., 9
Hersh, Seymour, 39
Higginbotham, A. Leon, Jr., 97
Hirschfield, Mary, 28, 31
Hodgson, Ray, 61
Hoffa, Jimmy, 37
Hoke, Martin, 44, 81
Holbrooke, Richard, 49, 128
Hopkins, William R., 7, 20–21
Hopwood, Erie C., 6
Horn, Karen, 92
Howard, Nathaniel B., 23
Huey, Norma, 34
Hughes, Robert, 32

Ishiyama, Toaru, 65

Jackson, Jesse L., 49, 77
Jackson, Maynard, 38
Jacobs, Jane, 27
Jarrett, Valerie, 160
Johnson, Tom L., 3, 16, 17, 38
Jones, Harlell, 31
Jordan, Vernon, 37, 121

Kanter, Rosabeth Moss, 116
Károlyi, Mihály, 7
Keehan, Carol, 161
Kellner, Larry, 116

Kemp, Evan J., Jr., 76
Kennedy, Paul M., 69
Kennedy, Robert F., 29–30
Kennedy, Ted, 39
Kenny, Enda, 161
Kent, Rockwell, 24
Kidder, Tracy, 49, 125
Kiley, Dan, 85
Kim, Jim Yong, 121
King, Billie Jean, 140
Kirkpatrick, James J., 27
Kirkpatrick, Jeane, 41
Kissinger, Henry, 128
Klein, Kurt, 94–95
Kohn, Vilma, 36
Kucinich, Dennis, 38
Kuhn, Maggie, 73
Kỳ, Nguyễn Cao 37–38

Lafferty, John J., 15, 25–26
Lansbury, George, 7
LaPierre, Wayne, 153
Lausche, Frank J., 19, 32
Leathem, Barclay, 18
Lemann, Nicholas, 89
Leutner, W. G., 10
Lewis, John, 112
Lewis, Peter B., 125
Lincoln, James F., 15
Locher, Cyrus, 16
Locher, Ralph S., 19, 32
Louv, Richard, 137
Lovins, Amory, 125
Lowery, Joseph E., 39, 85
Lustig, Bob, 43, 44–45

Maddox, Lester, 38
Manji, Irshad, 161
Masaryk, Tomáš Garrigue, 10
Maschke, Maurice, 17, 20–21
Massey, Walter E., 100
McCarrick, Theodore, 50, 121
McDonough, William A., 114–15
McGovern, George S., 35
McGuinness, Martin, 113
McKay, Hugh, 158
McKinney, Wade H., 26
McKnight, William T., 22
McLarty, Thomas F., III, 46
McLaughlin, Mitchel
McNeil, Ronald S., 51, 92
Means, Russell, 37, 78–79
Mearns, Geoffrey, 108
Mearsheimer, John J., 141
Menninger, Karl, 15
Meredith, James, 39
Metzenbaum, Howard, 85, 86
Mikulski, Barbara, 37
Milken, Michael, 50, 116
Miller, Aaron David, 148
Minor, Norman S., 22
Modell, Art, 81
Monnett, James G., Jr., 9
Montagu, Ashley, 40
Morgan, Daniel E., 5, 6, 16, 21, 23, 24, 40
Morgenthau, Robert M., 109
Morris, Thomas W., 72
Morrow, Lance, 81
Moss, Otis, Jr., 93
Moulthrop, Dan, 51–53
Moustapha, Imad, 132
Mulcahy, Anne, 130–31

Mullen, Mike, 152
Mullins, Aimee, 157
Murray, Thomas H., 105
Muskie, Edmund S., 35

Ness, Eliot, 21
Newkirk, Ingrid E., 68
Newman, Joseph S., 16, 19, 32, 41
Norquist, Grover, 155, 160
North, Oliver, 76
Norton, Eleanor Holmes, 41
Notkin, Boris, 84

Oakar, Mary Rose, 81
Ockert, Paul, 13
O'Connor, Sandra Day, 58–59
Orozco, Johanna, 157

Pacifico, Larry, 65
Packard, Vance, 26
Parks, Rosa, 40
Patrick, Deval, 145
Paul, Ron, 64
Pearson, Drew, 15
Pei Min Xin, 66–67
Pelosi, Nancy, 49
Peñalosa, Enrique, 49
Phillips, Kevin, 137
Pianalto, Sandra, 129
Pickens, T. Boone, 41
Pickens, William, 11, 15
Pilla, Anthony M., 97
Plavsic, Biljana, 104
Podhoretz, Norman, 37
Pogue, David, 141
Pogue, Dick, 45, 46, 47, 48

Poling, Harold A., 73
Polk, Franklin A., 32
Porter, Michael, 117
Porter, Philip W., 22, 23, 40
Pound, Richard, 136
Pound, Roscoe, 11
Prejean, Helen, 146–47
Price, Lucy, 7
Putnam, Robert, 113

Quiñonez, Catalina, 50

Rahman, Hassan Abdel, 51, 118–19
Ramo, Roberta Cooper, 93
Raper, Jack, 9, 9n5, 10, 11, 12, 13, 15,
    22, 41
Ravitch, Diane, 161
Reagan, Ronald, 42, 62–63
Rehm, Diane, 101
Reich, Robert, 96
Remírez de Estenoz, Fernando, 100
Reno, Janet, 97
Reston, James B., 24
Reuss, Henry S., 31
Reynolds, Butch, 81
Rhee, Michelle, 156
Rhee, Syngman, 10
Rice, Condoleezza, 126–27
Rice, Susan E., 104
Richard, Ronn, 153
Richards, Cecile, 141
Ridge, Tom, 124
Rivers, Victor, 149
Rivlin, Alice, 121
Roberts, Cokie, 157
Roberts, H. Melvin, 4
Roberts, J. Milnor, 82–83

Roberts, Steve, 157
Robertson, Pat, 113
Robinson, Frank, 37
Robinson, Larry, 33
Rogers, Will, 109
Rohatyn, Felix, 41n14
Roizen, Michael, 153
Rokakis, Jim, 142–43
Romer, Christina, 152
Roosevelt, Franklin D., 10
Roosevelt, Theodore, 7
Rosenbaum, Sidney, 9
Russell, Harold John, 65
Rustin, Bayard, 61

Safire, William, 39
Sapp, Ben, 18
Satcher, David, 117
Scalia, Antonin, 48, 125
Schieffer, Bob, 93
Schlafly, Phyllis, 38
Schorr, Daniel, 40
Schultz, Connie, 133
Schwartz, Nathan A., 18
Selig, Bud, 88
Seltzer, Louis B., 23
Shalala, Donna, 141
Shapiro, Ezra Z., 34
Sharkey, Mary Anne, 44
Shockley, William, 38
Shriver, R. Sargent, 35
Shroeder, Patricia, 69
Shultz, George P., 35
Siegelstein, Louis E., 9
Signorile, Michelangelo, 80
Silver, Abba Hillel, 11, 15, 26

Silverman, Mervyn, 60

Silverman, William, 45

Simalane, Solly, 72

Simpson, Alan K., 46, 154–55

Sindell, David, 42

Smeal, Eleanor, 61

Smisek, Jeff, 116

Snyder, Hilda, 15

Solmonese, Joe, 149

Soros, George, 49, 129

Sousa, John Philip, 10

Speth, Gus, 65

Spock, Benjamin, 31

Stashower, Fred, 19

Steagall, Henry B., 15

Steffens, Lincoln, 4, 15

Steinbacher, Roberta, 34

Steinbrenner, George, 38

Steinem, Gloria, 41

Stephanopoulos, George, 89

Stewart, Alice, 68

Stinchcomb, William A., 9

Stokes, Carl B., 29, 32

Stokes, Louis, 106–7

Stone, I. F., 27

Strassmeyer, Mary, 39

Sununu, John, 65

Sweeney, John, 38, 96

Taft, Rick, 3n1, 40, 45, 46, 51

Taft, Seth C., 3n1, 29

Talbott, Strobe, 145

Tannen, Deborah, 117

Tarbell, Ida M., 11

Taylor, Susan, 105

Teare, George W., 12

Thomas, Helen, 109

Thomas, Lowell, 11

Thomas, Marlo, 73

Thome, Jim, 157

Thompson, Tommy, 48

Thomsen, Mark L., 10

Thorne, Tracy, 82–83

Thurmond, Strom, 27

Thurow, Lester, 74–75

Tober, Ron, 46, 47

Toole, F. X. (Jerry Boyd), 50, 117

Townsend, Kathleen Kennedy, 30n9, 49, 141

Traficant, James, 80

Trumka, Richard, 152

Tubbs Jones, Stephanie, 85

Turner, Ted, 158–59

Tutu, Desmond, 109

Udall, Morris, 38

Unger, Paul, 41

Vanik, Charles A., 31

Vierow, Frederick A., 31

Volcker, Paul, 141

Voinovich, George V., 42, 43

Wagner, Thomas E., 60

Walker, William O., 26–27

Wallace, George, 28–29

Wallace, Mike, 45

Walt, Stephen M., 141

Webster, William, 38

Weidenthal, Bud, 35–36

Weinberger, Caspar W., 80

Weissmann Klein, Gerda, 94–95

Welch, Robert H. W., Jr., 27–28

Welser-Möst, Franz, 121

Westwood, Jean M., 36

White, Michael R., 43, 69, 86

White, Robert J., 68

Whiteleather, Melvin K., 24

Whitlock, Brand, 6

Whitman, Christine Todd, 137

Widder, Milt, 32

Wilder, Douglas, 137

Wilkerson, Isabel, 157

Williams, Juan, 140

Wilson, Joseph, IV, 129

Witt, Peter, 7, 9, 12, 15, 17, 23, 40

Wolfowitz, Paul, 73

Woodcock, Leonard, 35

Ya'alon, Moshe, 136

Young, Harrison, 76

Young, James R., 24

Young, Stephen M., 19

Youngner, Stuart J., 101

Yzaguirre, Raul, 100

Zeineddine, Farid, 26

Zhou Wenzhong, 144

Zumwalt, Elmo R., 37

Zung, Thomas T. K., 47